MOUNTAIN BIKE GUIDE

Mountain Bike Guide
The Peak District &
Derbyshire

by

MIKE PEARCE

Published by The Ernest Press 1997
© Copyright Mike Pearce

ISBN 0 948153 48 2

British Library Cataloguing-in-Publication Data has been regis-
tered with the British Library in Wetherby and is available on
request.

Typeset by Askvik Språktjenester A/S, Norway
Printed by Martins the Printers

Disclaimer:

Whilst we have made every effort to achieve accuracy in the
production of material for use in this guide book, the author,
publishers and copyright owners can take no responsibility for:
trespass, irresponsible riding, any loss or damage to persons or
property suffered as a result of the route descriptions or advice
offered in this book.

The inclusion of a route in this guide does not guarantee that
the path/track will remain a right of way; if conflict with land-
owners occurs, please be polite and leave by the shortest available route, then check the situation with the relevant authority.

It is worthwhile, as a footnote to this disclaimer, to empha-
sise that riders should give way to both pedestrians and horse
riders, and should make every effort to warn others of their
presence.

ACKNOWLEDGEMENTS
I should especially like to thank **Dave Towndrow**, my good-humoured companion on most of these rides. His total enthusiasm for mountain biking in any conditions and his willingness to suffer the rides that did not make it into the book most definitely enhanced the pleasure of compiling and checking these routes.

I would also like to thank the following people whose help has been most valuable; **Paul Allsop** for his advice on first-aid and help checking the rides. **Karen Allsop** for assistance with checking the rides. **Martin Gorman** of Peak Design for expert technical help with computers and programs. **John Holdcroft** of Marin for stepping into the breach by supplying a bike to complete the research rides after my original bike (not a Marin) suffered catastrophic failure on Holy Moor. Duncan Wardrop of Redland Aggregates Ltd for kind permission to use the track above Dow Low Quarry. My wife **Rosemary Pearce** for introducing me to mountain biking in the first place and for support and encouragement during the writing of this guide. **Gordon Stainforth** for his generously given encouragement and advice.

Route Location

West Yorkshire

Holmfirth
10

Greater Manchester

Glossop
13
18 Penistone

South Yorkshire

8

9

Edale
23 Hayfield *12*

Whaley Bridge Hope

Sheffield

Cheshire

Buxton
1

22

Ashford *14* *6* *7* Chesterfield

11

16 *2* Bakewell
Longnor *Hartington* *3*

4 Matlock

Wirksworth *20*

Leek

5

Nottingham-shire

15

Ashbourne Ambergate

Derbyshire

Staffordshire

Shirley *19* Derby

Burton on Trent

N

Netherseal
17

Leicestershire

Key

County	——
Peak Park	········
Route Number	*1*

Warwick-shire

Contents

INTRODUCTION

Mountain Biking in the Peak District and Derbyshire

The region covered by the Peak District National Park and the county of Derbyshire is without doubt one of the finest areas of England to explore by mountain bike. It extends from the gentle, intricate farmland of the south to the stark and dramatic hills of the north where 'Great winds blow over miles and miles of ling and bog and black rock, and the curlews still go crying in that empty air as they did before the Romans came.' (J.B. Priestley) Varied landscapes, secluded villages, quiet pubs and a long and complex history all combine to make riding in this part of the country a continually interesting and constantly surprising experience.

The first and probably the busiest in the country, the Peak District National Park receives millions of visitors each year. Notwithstanding this fact, it is likely that you will meet few other people, and possibly none at all, on the off-road sections of these rides. Many visitors stay close to the roads or converge on the 'honey pot' areas.

Whilst there is no doubt that the Park offers some exquisitely beautiful countryside, there are large areas of Derbyshire outside the Park that have equally interesting and varied landscapes. Indeed, Western Derbyshire and the White Peak contain some of Derbyshire's best kept secrets. I hope that this guide will help you discover some of these hidden and secluded parts that you might otherwise miss.

About this guide

This book describes circular rides in Derbyshire and the Peak District National Park. The routes cover the whole length and breadth of the area. Rides of all levels of difficulty are covered, from short and easy introductory rides to long and challenging rides over high hills. The careful descriptions and clear sketchmaps will make navigation straightforward.

The sketchmaps in this guide give a general picture of the routes but, although each map is roughly to scale, they are not all drawn to the same scale. They are designed to be used in conjunction with a 1:25 000 scale Ordnance Survey map (see Maps and Compasses section).

1

Rides do change with time: large barns appear overnight, bridleways are re-routed and quarries expand or are filled in. If you are unsure of your position or the way forward, consult your OS map.

Some features, for example gates or walls, are mentioned in the text and shown on the sketchmaps only when they are necessary for navigation. If a junction is not mentioned, follow the most obvious way on.

It will usually be possible to ride all of the routes as described. However there are some sections of some rides which may defeat all but the fittest and most able riders. Be prepared for short sections of pushing and even the occasional carry.

Where a route can be accessed from a railway station it is mentioned in the route information.

It is possible to start many of these rides at points other than those recommended, and to vary the routes according to taste. Doing a route in reverse will make it seem like a completely different ride. However please only ride where you have the legal right to do so.

Rights of way

Rights of way, and who and what can use them, are complex and much debated subjects in Derbyshire at the moment. The situation on the ground is not always clear and the absence of up-to-date definitive maps does not help. The generally accepted rules are as follows:

* Cyclists may not ride over footpaths, although you may push or carry your bike on a footpath. Not all footpaths are rights of way.
* Cyclists may ride over bridleways or tracks of higher status, for example RUPP – Road Used As Public Path, and BOAT – Byway Open To All Traffic. However they should give way to pedestrians and equestrians.
* Cyclists may ride over unclassified country roads, some of which may not be metalled. These are sometimes called 'White Roads'.
* The term 'Green Lane' – which has no legal meaning – usually refers to a walled track which may have some historical associations and may or may not be a right of way.

While comprehensive efforts have been made to ensure that the routes in this guide follow legal rights of way for cyclists, it is possible that mistakes have been made or that the status of a route has changed. The inclusion in this guide of a route, or indeed the marking of a right of way on an Ordnance Survey map, is no guarantee that you have current legal permission to use it. If you are challenged as to your right to be where you are, be polite and ask where the correct route is. A friendly, non-confrontational approach will often work wonders. If this fails, apologise and leave by the shortest practical route if requested to do so. You can check the legal classification of a right of way on the Definitive Map, and its subsequent variation orders which may be found at County Hall in Matlock. Please contact the author if you come across any major changes or problems.

Please treat the area with the respect it deserves. Ride carefully without intimidating other slower-moving visitors with noise, speed and large groups. The initially strong anti-mountain bike publicity has largely died down, due to both familiarity and responsible riding. Please do your bit to keep it this way!

ASSESSING THE RIDE

Your experience plus careful reading of the descriptions and details of length and timing of the rides should give you sufficient information to decide whether a ride is suitable for the ability of your party in the prevailing weather and surface conditions. It is recommended that you read the whole route description thoroughly, and study the map, before departure.

If you are a less experienced rider or a newcomer to the area, I suggest you start with the shorter and lower routes. Once you have completed a couple of these you should be able to assess how your abilities match up to the routes.

The times given are for an 'average' party stopping occasionally for food, etc. Be aware that times can vary greatly depending on surface conditions, weather and the party's fitness. Be prepared to cut your ride short if *anyone* in your party is struggling.

The distances given for each ride and for parts of a ride must be taken as approximations. The routes have been measured by two separate milometers and by map measurer, but these methods rarely produce the same result – even when repeated.

EQUIPMENT

Maps and compasses

I strongly recommend that you carry the appropriate 1:25 000 scale Ordnance Survey map when on the ride. Whilst you may rarely use your OS map for navigation, it will enable you to regain the correct route if you do lose the way or allow you to make detours from the main route to tempting pubs, etc.

Most of the rides are covered on either OS Outdoor Leisure Sheet 1 *Dark Peak* or 24 *White Peak*. Some rides are not covered by older versions of the White and Dark Peak maps – check before you leave home!

Details of the map or maps required are given at the start of each ride. Smaller scale maps (1:50 000 or 1 inch: 1 mile) do not show sufficient detail for accurate navigation. For your safety and for added interest it is recommended that you learn to interpret OS maps.

Six-figure grid references are used to locate the starts and some other key points on the routes.

It is worth investing in a plastic laminated map or a good map case. Unprotected paper maps quickly disintegrate in wet and windy conditions.

If you carry a map, carry a compass – and know how to use it! Remember that a large ferrous metal object (for example a steel-framed mountain bike) may affect a compass reading. Walk away from your bike when taking a bearing. Any compass directions given in the text are magnetic, i.e. they do not need correcting for magnetic variation – the difference between grid north and magnetic north.

Which bike?

You do not need to invest in the latest, most expensive mountain bike to do these rides. Many of them could be done on a basic machine, but there is no doubt that riding a purpose-built, lightweight and well-designed and equipped mountain bike means you will be less tired, have more fun and do less walking. When it comes to pushing or carrying, a lightweight bike is a definite plus.

I suggest you consider durability, total weight and equipment specification when choosing a bike. Go to a number of good specialist bike shops and ask questions. They are usually keen bikers themselves who will want to share their expertise and enthusiasm with you.

FIRST-AID

This is not the place for a comprehensive first-aid manual. Whilst serious injury is rare some fore-knowledge may help to prevent a minor accident turning into a serious incident. The following notes are intended as a guide to handling the sort of incident you are likely to come across on a ride.

1. Do not panic. Stay calm. Rushing around hysterically only makes the situation worse.
2. Take charge. Start organising the incident and the other people in your party.
3. Assess the situation. Is the casualty still in danger? Is anyone else in your party likely to be in danger? Do not move the casualty, especially if there is any likelihood of a back or neck injury. How serious is the injury? Give any first-aid you can.
4. Send for help, making sure you write down your exact location, giving the grid reference and the direction and distance from the nearest village or identifiable feature, together with your assessment of the injury. Ideally, in a party of four in an isolated situation, one person should stay with the casualty and two should go for help. Those who go for help should be aware that they must take extra care or you may be dealing with two incidents. The sooner professional help arrives the less serious your situation.
5. Make the casualty warm and comfortable. Reassure them that everything is under control and that they are going to be OK.

SAFETY ON THE HILLS

Mountain biking in high hills requires as much preparation and caution as hill walking. The northern part of the Peak District can be a very wild place even in summer. In winter, when days are short and the mist comes down, you may find yourself in a survival situation if you are not adequately prepared.

Take good, warm, waterproof and windproof clothing, including gloves and a hat or balaclava you can wear under your helmet. A lightweight plastic survival bag is very useful and may even save somebody's life one day. Wear good boots not training shoes; if you suffer a major technical problem you may have to carry or push your bike for some distance over rough or boggy terrain.

Take plenty of food and water with you. Always wear a helmet when riding. Keep your bike well-maintained and in good condition. Always carry spare inner tubes, a pump and an adequate tool kit.

Make sure somebody knows where you are going and what time you expect to return.

CONTACTING THE AUTHOR

If you need to contact the author to notify problems or changes, or just wish to share your experiences, please write to Mike Pearce c/o The Ernest Press, 595 Clarkston Road, Glasgow, G44 3QD, or direct via email: mpearce@globalnet.co.uk. Major changes or new information will be posted in the Usenet newsgroup: uk.rec.cycling. If you would like to be notified of any changes or updates via email (only) please send a blank email to mpearce@globalnet.co.uk with the word 'update' in the subject field.

The trusty steed

1 Ashford & Deep Dale

Priestcliffe

The Waterloo ■ A6

N

1 kilometre

A515

Barn ■

Bull-i'-th'-Thorn

High Peak Trail

Monyas

A515

High Dale

Brushfield

Monsal Trail

Monsal Head

Hotel

B6465

River Wye

A6

Car Park

Deep Dale

Start

Car Park

Ashford

Dalehouse Farm

b

Route	- - - - - -
Track	= = = = =
Road	———
Canal	– – – –
River	▓▓▓▓▓
Stream	———
Footpath	·········
Field	———

1. Ashford & Deep Dale

Distance	29 km, 18 miles, 62% off-road.
Time	3 hours.
Map	OS Outdoor Leisure 24 *White Peak*.
Facilities	Café at Monsal Head. Pubs along the route. Shops and pubs in Ashford.
Rail Access	Not practical.

Summary

A great route that ascends to Monsal Head before descending into Monsal Dale and climbing again to traverse the high limestone plateau of central Derbyshire. A short section of the High Peak Trail and a fast track bring you to the outskirts of Monyash. The ride ends with the descent of steep-sided Deep Dale. This route stays high for some time and is therefore exposed to the weather.

The Route

Start from carpark in **Ashford**, OS grid ref. 195698. (If this small carpark is full an alternative start can be made from the carpark at the lower end of Deep Dale, OS grid ref. 170706. However this carpark closes at dusk.) Directions are given from the Ashford carpark.

Emerge from the carpark to turn right and ascend a minor road to a junction with the **B6465**. Turn left onto the B6465, then climb steadily for 1.5 km to **Monsal Head**. Turn left immediately after the **Monsal Head Hotel**. Follow the road down to the floor of the valley. Take the first track on the left that cuts back to a farm. Immediately before the farm turn right and cross a footbridge over the **River Wye**.

On the far side of the bridge take the narrow path that ascends diagonally leftwards, avoiding the wider track beside the river. Climb this rocky path to a bridlegate that gives access to the **Monsal Trail**.

Cross straight over, passing through another bridlegate, signposted *Brushfield.* Beyond the gate keep to the right and climb the overgrown rubble path. After 50 metres, at a more open section, keep to the right again to enter a walled continuation of the path. This soon becomes less 'technical' and it is possible to remount! The path joins a wider track at a sweeping bend. Follow this track straight on (yet more rubble) still ascending towards the brow of the hill.

Stay on this track as it meanders pleasantly across open fields to a junction marked by a wooden fingerpost. Go straight on, signposted *Brushfield*, to enter the top of a small dale. Follow the wide track to **Brushfield**.

Pass through the hamlet to a minor road. Turn left and follow the tarmac down for 400 metres to a sharp left-hand bend in the road. Leave the road here by passing through a narrow squeeze on the right onto a grassy bridleway that follows the bottom of **High Dale**. Ride easily through this steep-sided valley, keeping the wall to your right. Where the wall ends at a corner, turn right and follow the vague grassy track up to, and through, a small narrow cutting. Follow this small depression, ascend the field, then pass through a gap in a tumbledown section of the wall on the left and over a stile to reach a track.

Turn left and follow the track round a sharp left-hand bend. Go left again at the next junction where a track joins from the right. Ascend to **Priestcliffe**.

Ride through Priestcliffe, join a minor road and continue to a fork. Take the right fork. You should pass a postbox on the left, 20 metres along this road. Continue over a crossroads to reach a T-junction with the A6 by **The Waterloo** public house.

Cross over this busy road with care and take the track to the left of the pub. Follow this gravel track up the scarp face, round a sharp left-hand bend and into a walled track. Cross the limestone plateau by following this track to a T-junction with a minor road.

Turn right. Ignore the first minor road on the left. Keep left at the next junction, signposted *Chelmorton*. Go straight across a minor road to enter a broad track. Follow this flat and fast track to its end at a minor road.

11

Turn left and ride to a T-junction with the **A515**. Turn right, signposted *Buxton*, and ride for 200 metres before turning left and descending a wide, walled and grassy track signposted *High Peak Trail*. After 300 metres, and at the bottom of the slope, turn left through a bridlegate onto the **High Peak Trail**.

Follow the trail for 2.4 km to **Hurdlow Carpark** (marked Sparklow on the OS map). Leave the trail here by riding out onto the road on the left. Follow this road rightwards, east, to a crossroads with the **A515**. Turn left and ride for 600 metres to just before the **Bull-i'-th'-Thorn Hotel**. Turn right immediately before (south-east of) the camping field adjacent to the hotel into a broad gravel track.

This track – Hutmoor Butts – gives an enjoyable, fast descent to a track crossroads. Go straight across and then veer right, passing into another walled track for more of the same. This track ends at a minor road near **Dalehouse Farm**.

Turn left and follow the minor road north. Ignore the first minor road on the left. At the T-junction turn right and after 150 metres turn right again at a crossroads, signposted *Sheldon & Ashford*. Ride along for 1 km with the narrow defile of Deep Dale gradually coming into view on your left. Turn left on a bridleway signposted *Deep Dale & Taddington Dale*.

Descend the broad grassy track to a left-hand bend in a dip. Go right through a gate, signposted *Public Bridleway*, to enter the upper part of **Deep Dale**. Ride down the dale, keeping a wall to your right, and then passing through a gate in the wall to continue on the other side of the wall. Although not steep, this descent is not quite as easy as it looks!

Towards the lower end of the dale the path forks. Take the right fork that ascends over a low saddle. (This avoids the extremely narrow, cave-like lower section of the dale – which is worth exploring but only on foot.) After the saddle follow the grassy track round to the right and contour across the hillside to a rocky path junction by hawthorn trees.

Go down and left following a path signposted *Bridleway to A6* that curves back on itself. Go down this rocky path and pass through

A lightweight bike is a definite plus. Carrying up Cave Dale.

a narrow cleft between two small crags to reach a low wall with a stone-stepped stile. Do not go over the wall, but instead turn right and descend the muddy and boulder-strewn bed of the lower part of Deep Dale. Where the dale opens out into a field, go right and contour along the hillside ignoring the more obvious path that goes straight on towards a stone-lined culvert. Ride for 200 metres before crossing the field diagonally leftwards to a gate onto the **A6**.

Turn right and ride for 2.3 km to a minor road on the left signposted *Ashford*. Turn left and ride for 500 metres back to **Ashford** village and the carpark.

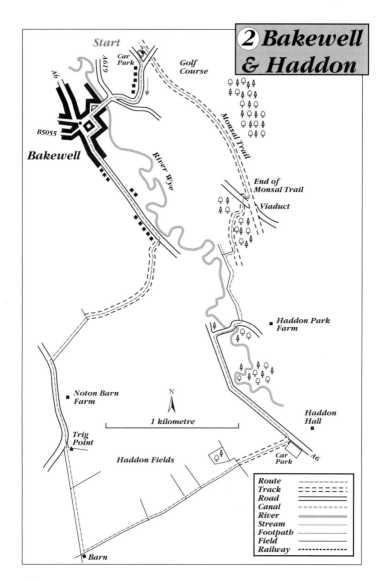

Start

Car Park

A6

A619

Golf Course

B5055

Bakewell

River Wye

Monsal Trail

End of Monsal Trail

Viaduct

Haddon Park Farm

Noton Barn Farm

N

1 kilometre

Haddon Hall

Trig Point

Haddon Fields

Car Park

A6

Barn

Route	----------
Track	========
Road	————
Canal	— — — —
River	————
Stream	————
Footpath	··········
Field	
Railway	-·-·-·-·-

2. Bakewell and Haddon

Distance	10 km, 6 miles, 70% off-road.
Time	1 hour.
Map	OS Outdoor Leisure 24 *White Peak*.
Facilities	Shops, pubs and cafés in Bakewell.
Rail Access	Not practical.

Summary

This ride is a good and enjoyable introduction if you are new to off-road biking or if you want a pleasant, short evening ride. It is straightforward with no navigational or technical problems. The route starts from Bakewell, climbs gently up to Haddon Fields, then descends to Haddon Hall and ambles back to Bakewell via the Monsal Trail.

The Route

Start in the carpark for the Monsal Trail by the disused Bakewell Station on the north-eastern outskirts of **Bakewell**. OS grid ref. 222690.

To find the carpark from the centre of Bakewell follow the A619 eastwards across the famous stone bridge over the River Wye. As the road curves left on leaving the bridge, take Station Road – the B6408 – rightwards, signposted *Industrial Estate*. Follow this road for 400 metres to find the carpark (signposted) by the old station building.

To start the ride leave the carpark by riding down Station Road and crossing over the stone bridge heading for Bakewell town centre. A few metres after the bridge turn left immediately after the **Queen's Arms** pub. Follow this unnamed road round past the site of the famous market to a T-junction with the A6, south of the town centre.

Turn left and ride along the **A6**. On the right after about 900 metres, a track leaves the road. The track is signposted *Public Bridleway To Over Haddon* and is just past the last of the houses on the right-hand side of the road.

Ride up the track to a field. Go straight on up the field. Pass through a small, but substantial, metal gate to a minor road. Turn left and ride along to a sharp right-hand bend at the crest of a small hill, approximately 3.8 km from the start of the ride. A bridleway goes straight on into a large field.

Enter the large field through the wide gate just to the right of the chevron road sign. Go straight on, riding beside the dry-stone wall on the right-hand side of the field. Enter a second field and keep going straight on, crossing **Haddon Fields**, towards a **barn** by a small copse.

In the corner by the barn, turn left within the same field, and ride eastwards alongside another dry-stone wall. In wet conditions it is best to avoid this swampy corner by cutting diagonally across to the left before you reach the barn. Please offer assistance to other mountain bikers who may have attempted a direct crossing. Ropes, etc., may be useful.

Follow the trackless fields, always beside the wall, down towards Haddon Hall which will soon be seen low on the opposite hillside. Join a stony track with small rocky steps that ends beside the **Haddon Hall** carpark on the A6.

Turn left and ride along the **A6** for 1 km. Then, at a point approximately 7.4 km from the start, turn right into a tarmac drive signposted *Haddon Park Farm*. Ride along the drive, crossing the **River Wye**. Just before the next right-hand bend take the bridleway, signposted *Public Bridleway To Coombs Road*, in the field on the left.

Follow narrow paths to the end of the first field. Do not cross into the second field, but instead turn right and ascend to a narrow gate and a gravel track. Turn left and follow the track for 200 metres to a small tarmac lane by a stone **viaduct** that once carried the Matlock to Buxton railway line. Go more or less straight across to climb a steep narrow path up to the old railway line; now called the **Monsal Trail**.

Near Haddon Hall.

Turn left and ride northwards along the Trail for 1.3 km to **Bakewell Station**. This is just after the second bridge over the Trail where the trail widens and a distinctive stone building – the old station – backs onto the Trail. Leave the Trail by passing to the north of the old station buildings to emerge in the carpark where you started your ride.

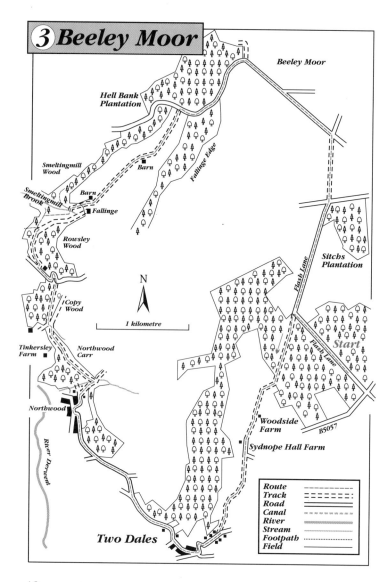

3 Beeley Moor

Beeley Moor

Hell Bank
Plantation

Smeltingmill
Wood

Barn

Fallinge Edge

Smeltingmill
Brook

Barn

Fallinge

Rowsley
Wood

Sitchs
Plantation

Flash Lane

N

Copy
Wood

1 kilometre

Tinkersley
Farm

Northwood
Carr

Flash Lane

Start

Northwood

River Derwent

Woodside
Farm

B5057

Sydnope Hall Farm

Two Dales

Route	– – – – –
Track	=====
Road	=====
Canal	– – – –
River	
Stream	
Footpath	....
Field	

18

3. Beeley Moor

Distance	14 km, 9 miles, 50% off-road.
Time	1 hour.
Map	OS Outdoor Leisure 24 *White Peak*.
Facilities	Pub in Two Dales.
Rail Access	Matlock Station (4 km from Two Dales).

Summary

A short, but varied and interesting ride, starting high on the moors above Darley Dale, descending into the Derwent Valley and climbing out via an intricate route that contains a short (but avoidable) 'technical' section, i.e. a carry! The woodland sections along the valley sides are excellent.

The Route

Start in **Flash Lane** at or near the bend at OS grid ref. 293654. Flash Lane is the minor road that leaves the B5057 approximately 3.5 km north-east of Darley Dale. Park either in one of the pull-ins beside the road in the plantation south-east of the bend or at the bend itself, where a bridleway leaves the road. Be careful not to block any access tracks.

From the bend in **Flash Lane** take the sandy track south-south-west through the plantation, passing the barred entrance to Whitehaven Forest after a few hundred metres. Follow the track straight on until it becomes tarmac for a short section just after **Woodside Farm**. Where the tarmac turns sharp left, carry straight on down the walled, tree-lined track. This track provides an interesting descent as it becomes steeper and rougher before it ends by a cattle grid on the outskirts of **Two Dales**.

Drop down and left for a few metres to join the **B5057**. Turn right, downhill, and negotiate the sharp bends. Immediately after the third and last bend, turn right into an unnamed minor road. This is immediately opposite Lady Grove Road.

Go straight on passing the Plough Inn to reach, after 300 metres, a T-junction with Hallmoor Road. Turn right and ride up Hallmoor Road ignoring Moor Lane on the left. Hallmoor Road ends at another T-junction with a high gritstone wall directly opposite. Turn left and ride down a few metres to a T-junction. Turn right and ride uphill to reach Lumb Lane on the right. Lumb Lane has a name board and a dead-end sign to identify it. Ride up the lane, ignoring the first bridleway on the left, signposted *Tinkersley*. (The signpost is hidden in a hawthorn tree on the right of the entrance to the bridleway.) Carry straight on up to take the grassy bridleway signposted *Rowsley-Ashover Road*.

Follow the bridleway steeply up for a hundred metres. Just past a small disused quarry and below the wall at the top of the wood, reach a path junction. Turn left to pass over the out-fall of a stream culvert and take the wide path downhill. Follow this excellent path through **Northwood Carr** to its end at a gate.

Passing through the gate, follow the track straight on. After a few metres, go through a second gate on the right and then, almost immediately, through a third gate on the left and into a wood.

Climb gently through **Copy Wood**, following the path until it meets a road. Turn left and ride steeply down the tarmac through the sharp bends. Two hundred and fifty metres after the last bend and just past a house on the right, turn right into a farm track, signposted *Haddon Estate*.

Follow the track through **Rowsley Wood** for 300 hundred metres to a point where it levels off and a low wooden post with a blue bridleway arrow is seen on the left. Leave the farm track here.

Follow the narrow path as it drops down to the left from the track, then almost immediately take the path right by another wooden post and follow it deeper into the woods. Keep to the right at a fork where a footpath continues more steeply down to the left. A very small stream crosses the path after which the bridleway starts to ascend and becomes less well-defined.

Keeping the deep, block-filled gully on your left, follow the path as it climbs the bank becoming steeper and more difficult as it ascends. Eventually the path deteriorates to a short section of steep, muddy steps. This is probably not rideable. Carry your bike up, paralleling the bottom of the gully, to reach a narrow wooden footbridge that crosses the stream. Go over the bridge and follow the path round to the right to a gate into a field. (This short section can be avoided by crossing the boulder-strewn stream bed via a vague path approximately 15 metres below the bridge. However this is just as awkward and perhaps even more slippery.)

Follow the left wall of the field, heading for the black, iron-roofed barn. Pass the right side of the barn and follow the obvious wide and muddy track north-eastwards. The track crosses fields until it meets tarmac on the minor road that rises eastwards from Beeley.

Turn right and follow the road up past **Hell Bank Plantation** towards **Beeley Moor**. Go round the sharp right-hand bend at the top and continue straight on, passing a minor road on the left, until reaching a crossroads formed by a second minor road on the left and a wide rough track on the right. If you are lucky, a tea and ice-cream van will welcome you to the highest point of the ride, 339 metres ASL.

After you have refreshed yourself take the wide track left that leaves the crossroads in a roughly southerly direction. Follow this track to another crossroads. Continue straight over into **Flash Lane**. Weave and undulate pleasantly along the tarmac to the start of the bridleway where you began the ride.

Rowsley Wood

Near Fallinge. (opp.)

4 Bonsall Moor

Ruin ■

Quarry

Bonsall Moor

Top Hill Farm

Whitelow Farm

Grangemill

N

1 kilometre

Griffe Grange

High Peak T

Water Tank

Hopton Incline

Tunnel

Mi

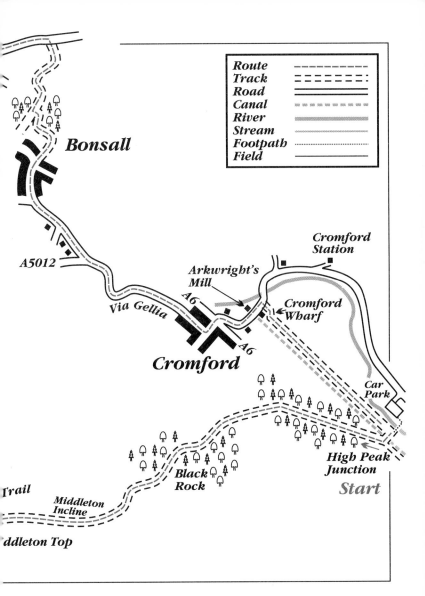

4. Bonsall Moor

Distance	21 km, 13 miles, 76% off-road.
Time	2 hours.
Map	OS Outdoor Leisure 24 *White Peak*.
Facilities	Shops and pubs in Bonsall and Cromford plus a café at Cromford Wharf and High Peak Junction.
Rail Access	Cromford Station (400 metres from Cromford Wharf.) Trains do not run every day.

Summary

The complex industrial past of Derbyshire is very evident on this route. The ride starts from the floor of the Derwent Valley and follows the long inclines of the disused Cromford & High Peak mineral railway (the High Peak Trail) to the limestone plateau at Griffe Grange. It descends to the Via Gellia and then crosses Bonsall Moor before descending into Bonsall and Cromford. It returns to High Peak Junction via the flat and easy Cromford Canal towpath.

The total height gain on the first section is 274 metres (nearly 900 feet) and although the going is easy the climbs are long. Another 97 metres (315 feet) are gained in the ascent to Bonsall Moor, but again the surface – mainly tarmac – is easy.

The Route

Start at **High Peak Junction** carpark which is just off the Cromford to Lea Bridge road at OS grid ref. 316561.

From the carpark take the gravel track in the south-west corner, cross three bridges and arrive at the Visitor Centre. Behind the Visitor Centre is the start of the **High Peak Trail** and the long climb out of the Derwent Valley. This climb – like all Gaul – is divided into three parts. The first and longest climb (Sheep Pasture Incline) begins immediately. Take a deep breath and start pedalling! The surface is good, the gradient even and the scenery pleasant. (Just after passing under the A6 road bridge a few metres after the start of the climb look out for a 'catch pit' with the wreckage of a railway truck still in it.)

At the top of the incline pass through a gate and continue along the High Peak Trail past an old winding house. Continue, passing Steeple Grange on your left, to the second climb, Middleton Incline, which ascends to **Middleton Top** where the winding house still contains the original steam engine used to haul trucks up the incline.

Ride on along the trail passing through two gates where a quarry track crosses your path. Shortly after this a limestone cutting leads to **Hopton Tunnel**. Go through the tunnel and then up Hopton Incline, the third and easiest climb.

Just after the top of the incline there is a house on the right. 50 metres past the house and also on the right is a gate into a field. Leave the High Peak Trail here (OS grid ref. 252546).

Go through the gate into the field. (This field can be identified by the final pylon of a power line.) Follow the left (west) wall of the field through a gate into a second field, and then via another gate into a third field which contains a water tank raised on a mound. The track continues in the same direction, but now with a wall on its right.

Where the track curves left go straight on through the gate. Follow the left wall down to another gate set into the wall in the corner. Go left through the gate and down the stony track to join a larger track by a cattle grid.

Go straight on, passing under the power lines. Where this track turns left and approaches **Griffe Walk Farm**, carry straight on in the same direction as the power lines. Follow this long, downhill track to two gates. Pass through the left-hand gate. Ride across the field, paralleling the right field boundary to a wooden gate where a footpath crosses your route. A wooden signpost marks this junction.

Pass through the gate and then go immediately right through a second gate. The bridleway follows the right boundary of the field for a few metres and then contours leftwards across the field, almost under the power lines, to pass through a gap in the overgrown field boundary. Follow the track to a gate and down to meet the A5012 Via Gellia at **Grangemill**.

Cross straight over and ride a few metres along the **B5056**, signposted *Bakewell*, and then turn right into a minor road, signposted *Ible*. Ride up this road keeping to the left at a fork. Climb through **Tophill Farm** to a crossroads and turn left. The tarmac soon gives way to gravel. Follow the wide track round a right-hand bend and continue over a road and across the bleak and eerie **Bonsall Moor**, the last place in Derbyshire to have a gibbet.

Go straight on, ascending to a left-hand bend. (Note – quarrying activity has changed the track layout and the OS map is no longer accurate.) After the bend, ascend the track for 50 metres. On the left is a ruined barn, on the right two huge metal gates. A few metres past the barn a broad, newly made gravel track branches off to the right. Go down this track to a more open area and then go slightly right into a more overgrown section. This ends at a widening of the track with a gate barring the way on.

Just to the left of the gate, hidden in the shrubs, is the narrow start of a path. Follow this path, which soon becomes slightly wider and grassy, straight on for about 500 metres to a minor road. Serious jungle hounds can go straight across into an even more overgrown – but short – section of path which cuts off the corner. Not recommended if you are wearing shorts! Alternatively turn right and then after a few metres, left into the minor road.

Follow this road. After 850 metres a footpath will be seen leaving the road on the right. Approximately 150 metres further on, and also on the right is a walled bridleway. Follow this bridleway into a field.

Follow the wall on the left round and down to a gate. Go through the gate and down into a 'tunnel' formed by trees overhanging the path. A few metres further on turn left and follow a similar narrow path slightly uphill.

This tricky path follows the edge of a small wood on the left and a field on the right. Continue to a path junction and then go right down an unusual concrete track to emerge near the cross in the centre of **Bonsall**.

Turn left and follow the main street through Bonsall and down for nearly a kilometre to a T-junction with the A5012, **Via Gellia** by the Holly Bush.

Approaching Grange Mill.

Turn left and follow this winding and steep-sided valley down to a T-junction in **Cromford**. Turn left and ride to the traffic lights at the staggered crossroads with the **A6**. Turn right, and then immediately left, signposted *Lee, Holloway, Crich*.

Pass **Arkwright's Mill** on your left. A few metres further on, but on your right, is the main carpark for **Cromford Wharf**, the northern end of the **Cromford Canal**. Turn into the main carpark. There is a café in the shop.

Follow the east bank of the canal southwards for 1.8 km to **High Peak Junction**. The canal towpath is a concessionary cycle-way and, especially at weekends, can be very busy with pedestrians and cyclists. Please ride slowly and give way to walkers. When you reach the wooden swing bridge by the Visitor Centre at **High Peak Junction**, turn left and retrace your tracks to the carpark.

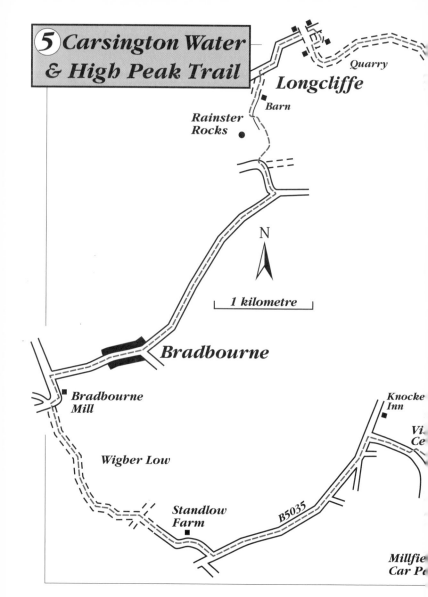

5 Carsington Water & High Peak Trail

Quarry

Longcliffe

Barn

Rainster Rocks

N

1 kilometre

Bradbourne

Knocke Inn

Bradbourne Mill

Vi
Ce

Wigber Low

Standlow Farm

B5035

Millfie
Car Pe

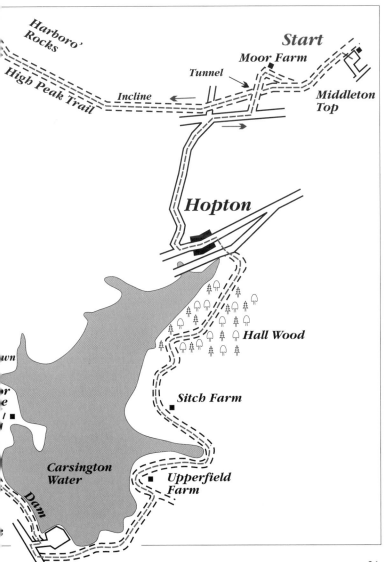

5. Carsington Water & High Peak Trail

Distance	30 km, 19 miles, 70% off-road.
Time	3 hours.
Map	OS Outdoor Leisure 24 *White Peak* (older editions do not show Carsington Water).
Facilities	Café at Carsington Water. Bike hire shop at Middleton Top and one at Carsington Water which also sells a few spares. Good pub *en route*.
Rail Access	Not practical.

Summary

A route of contrasts. It first follows a section of the High Peak Trail before descending through Bradbourne and crossing two bridleways to reach Carsington Water. It then uses the cycle-way round the south-east side of the reservoir, and finally returns to Middleton Top via Hopton. Although I must admit to a mild suspicion of prepared bike trails, the ride round the far side of Carsington Water has been thoughtfully constructed and is surprisingly attractive. It has a series of short climbs and one good descent. Altogether this is an unexpectedly good ride.

The Route

Start from the High Peak Trail carpark at **Middleton Top**, OS grid ref. 276552. From the carpark go out onto the **High Peak Trail**. Follow the Trail leftwards (west). Ride along the Trail passing over various tracks, through **Hopton Tunnel** and up **Hopton Incline**. Continue along the Trail and after approximately 5.5 km cross a bridge over a road. Continue round what on the High Peak Trail counts as a sharp right-hand bend then pass a small disused quarry on the left. A few hundred metres after the quarry reach the old **Longcliffe Station**, approximately 5.7 km from the start.

Leave the Trail here via a black tarmac track on the right just before a stone barn which is also on the right and is itself diagonally opposite a small terrace of houses on the left of the Trail. Follow the tarmac round a hairpin bend to pass through a gate onto the road.

Turn left. After passing round a left-hand and then a right-hand bend, take the signposted bridleway on the left. There is a small pond in the corner of the field to the right of the bridleway.

Ride for 150 metres to just before an old barn. Go right through a gap in the wall and follow the bridleway that passes to the west (right-hand) side of the wall (*not to the east as marked on older versions of the White Peak map*). Follow the bridleway through fields keeping the wall on your left until you reach a bridlegate (marked with a blue arrow) in the wall.

Go through the gate and turn right still following the wall. Follow the track out across the field passing beside **Rainster Rocks** then round to the right to where it meets a minor road at a bend. Ignore the track on the left, but take the tarmac road to the left that climbs gently.

At a T-junction turn right, signposted *Bradbourne*. A short ascent then a long descent takes you through **Bradbourne**. Ignore the minor road, signposted *Carsington & Kniveton*, that joins from the left in Bradbourne. Continue down through Bradbourne to reach a T-junction with the B5056. Turn left, signposted *Ashbourne & Fenny Bentley*.

Ride for a couple of hundred metres. On the left, opposite a minor road that leads to **Tissington Ford** and just after the right-hand bend by **Bradbourne Mill**, an obvious track climbs straight on up the hillside. Ascend the rutted track to emerge into a field. Strike diagonally left across the field to find a gate by a large, dead tree on the opposite side. Do not take the more obvious grassy track that appears to go straight on and passes just to the left of the house.

Follow this wooded track to a field. Cross the field keeping a wall at first to your left and then to your right. Follow this wall straight on across fields, always keeping it on your right, to find a gate in a corner by hawthorn trees. Pass through the gate into a larger field.

From here the route goes down and slightly left by a line of trees that mark the course of an old hedge. At the lower edge of the field follow the fence left to a gate in the corner. Go through the gate and follow the path to the right of a large barn. Pass through the small farmyard and continue straight on up the gravel drive to a minor road.

Go straight across into a field. Ride up the field next to the right-hand boundary, then cross two more fields to reach a small tarmac lane at a bend. Turn left and ride past **Standlow Farm** to a T-junction with the **B5035**. Turn left and ride along the road for 2 km.

At a point approximately 16 km from the start turn right into a minor road, signposted *Carsington Water, Hulland Ward & Atlow*. (If you carry straight on here you can visit the **Knockerdown Inn** which is a few meters along on the right.)

A couple of hundred metres along the Carsington Water road, take the gravel path on the left that at first parallels the road and then branches off to the left, cutting off the corner of the **Carsington Water** access road. The gravel track joins the tarmac for a few metres – go left. Just before the T-junction a prepared gravel path crosses the road. Go right and ride beside the carparks towards the sailing club.

Cross the access road to the sailing club to join a wider, better gravel track, signposted *Millfields & Horse Trail*. Follow this track round to the start of the dam itself.

Go straight over the earth-bank dam (which collapsed during construction). At the far side follow paved paths into the carpark at **Millfields**. Turn right and go out the carpark entrance to the road. Turn left and ride uphill for a few metres to the start of the way-marked cycle-route on the left. Follow this round Carsington Water. This part of the ride is not shown on the OS *White Peak* map. This should not be a problem; the cycle-route is quite easy to follow.

Take care on the blind bends; this is a popular area and, especially during holidays and at weekends, many young or inexperienced cyclists will be trundling slowly along. There are a couple of places where the route is not immediately obvious:

Where the track joins a sunken lane, turn left to ride down the lane to the continuation of the cycle-route on the right.

Carsington Reservoir.

Just before **Upperfield Farm** turn left, signposted *Hopton Village* (good lunch spot), and ride down to a tarmac lane. Turn left and go down past the farm. Ignore the track immediately after the farm and ride on for a few metres to the signposted continuation of the cycle-way on the right.

Follow the cycle-way as it undulates smoothly round the reservoir. After one particularly steep ascent followed by a pleasant woodland descent, the path curves round to meet the **B5035** at the north-eastern corner of the reservoir. Cross straight over the road and go up a short gravel track, signposted *Hopton Village*, to a minor road.

Turn left and ride through **Hopton Village**. After leaving the village take the first road on the right (not signposted). Climb steadily to a crossroads. Turn right, signposted *Wirksworth*, and ride to the brow of the hill. Take the tarmac farm track on the left. The track becomes gravel before curving round to the right past **Moor Farm**. A few hundred metres past Moor Farm, the track crosses the High Peak Trail. Turn left (east) along the Trail and ride back to Middleton Top.

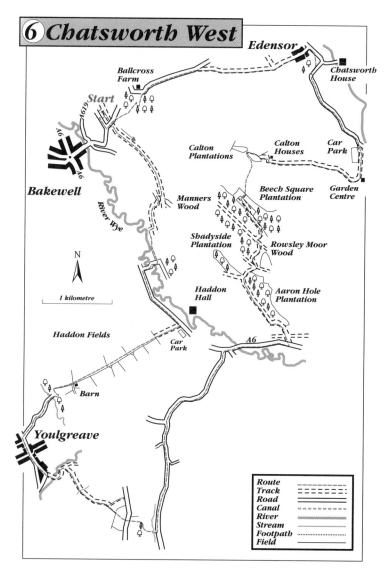

6 Chatsworth West

Edensor

Chatsworth House

Ballcross Farm

Start

A619

A6

Bakewell

A6

River Wye

Calton Plantations

Calton Houses

Car Park

Manners Wood

Beech Square Plantation

Garden Centre

N

1 kilometre

Shadyside Plantation

Rowsley Moor Wood

Haddon Hall

Aaron Hole Plantation

Haddon Fields

Car Park

A6

Barn

Youlgreave

Route	....
Track	
Road	
Canal	
River	
Stream	
Footpath	
Field	

6. Chatsworth West

Distance	24 km, 15 miles, 75% off-road.
Time	3 hours.
Map	OS Outdoor Leisure 24 *White Peak*.
Facilities	Shops and pubs in Bakewell and Youlgreave.
Rail Access	Not practical.

Summary

An excellent and interesting ride with some relatively big climbs and a tricky, technical (but short) descent. The ride starts in the market town of Bakewell, traverses the valleys of three major rivers of central Derbyshire and the parkland surrounding Chatsworth House and Haddon Hall.

The Route

Start in the carpark for Monsal Trail by the disused Bakewell Station on the north-eastern outskirts of **Bakewell** at OS grid ref. 222690. To find the carpark from the centre of Bakewell follow the A619 across the famous stone bridge over the River Wye, to the east of the town centre. As the road curves left on leaving the bridge, take the minor road – the B6408 – rightwards, signposted *Industrial Estate*. Follow this road for 400 metres to find the carpark signposted on the left.

Leave the carpark at the far corner by the old station buildings to join the **Monsal Trail**. Turn right, south-eastwards, pass under a stone bridge and ride for 1.3 km until a wooden fence barring the way on marks the end of the trail. On the right, a few metres before the fence, a narrow path drops steeply down to tarmac. Turn left, then immediately right, to take the left-hand of the two gravel tracks. The right-hand of these two tracks has a gate with a sign *Landscape Forestry*. Ignore this track. Ride along the left-hand track for a couple of hundred metres until, on the right, a signposted bridleway leaves the track via a bridlegate into a field. The bridleway is not well-marked on the ground. Follow the right-hand fence down to the lower edge of the field and then turn left to ride southwards beside the **River Wye**. At the end of the field pass through a bridlegate and turn right along tarmac to reach the A6 road. Turn left and ride along for 1 km until just before the carpark at **Haddon Hall**. To the right, north, of the carpark a gate with a low, stone stile on its left gives access to a bridleway, signposted *Youlgreave*.

Pass through a second gate and climb the track which is naturally paved with Carboniferous Limestone. Climb steadily through fields, at first on a gravel track and then over grass, always keeping roughly to the same line, but with one minor detour through a gate. Eventually reach a barn by a copse. In the wet it is best to avoid the disgusting mire by a detour out to the right to come back left, crossing into the next field a few metres north of the barn via a bridlegate in the tumbledown wall. A signpost, *Bridleroad Youlgreave*, points the way on. Cross the field in roughly the same direction you have been travelling. On the far side of the field pass through a bridlegate, signposted *Public Bridleway*, found in the angle formed by a wooden fence on the left and a stone wall on the right.

Follow the obvious path through a gap in a bank and immediately begin an excitingly steep and narrow descent with very sharp bends and drop-offs. If you are not fully confident of your downhill technique, it would be wise to walk this section. At the bottom cross a narrow stone bridge over the **River Lathkill**. Keep a lookout for large trout basking in the pools. Continue straight on, climbing to meet a minor road. Turn left and ride to the crossroads by the church in the centre of **Youlgreave**.

Go straight over the crossroads into Bradford Road. Where the road forks, keep to the left. Approximately 150 metres after the fork, just where the road curves to the right, take the bridleway to the left of **Braemar House** and down a narrow walled path to cross a narrow bridge over the **River Bradford**. Follow the tarmac track left, and then right, up and away from the river. Continue on the tarmac, crossing a track, passing **Lower Greenfields** and on towards a second farm (unnamed on the OS map). The tarmac track becomes gravel and, immediately after the farm, curves left. Leave the track here, crossing the field parallel to the right-hand field boundary to reach a gate hidden in the corner of the field.

Continue in the same direction across the next field. Cross over the minor road and through a bridlegate. On the far field boundary are four prominent trees. Head for the one on the left. Just to the left of this tree, pass through a gate and down a short narrow path. The path opens out and curves down to cross **Ivy Bar Brook** at a double-gated bridge. Ride up the field to reach the road, the B5056, via a bridlegate in the top right-hand corner. Turn left and follow the road for 1.5 km to a T-junction. Turn right and then, after another 1.4 km, right again on the **A6**.

Ride along the A6 for 900 metres. At a point approximately 13 km from the start of the ride, turn left on a gravel track. This track passes under a low power line and through a gap in an old railway embankment. Climb steadily past **Aaron Hole Plantation** until, just after cresting the hill, you reach a bridleway T-junction. Turn right, signposted *Bakewell*, and ride down – then up – to another junction.

The path straight across, through a gap in the wall and signposted *Bridlepath Chatsworth*, is the way on. Climb diagonally leftwards up the hillside. The path soon turns right, becomes steeper and climbs through woods to join a track which contours across the hillside. Turn left and ride along for a few metres to a junction marked by a low post. Turn right and climb steeply through the woods. The track eventually curves left, levels off and is bounded on its right side by a high, dry-stone wall. Ride along by the wall to reach an opening marked by two large stone pillars.

Pass through the gap, then turn left, north-westwards. Meander pleasantly through flat, open woodland led on by an occasional bridleway marker. Emerge from the trees into a more open area and head for the far right-hand corner. Pass over a tumbledown wall to the right of a wooden gate, then ride down through a short section of trees to a double gate with a stile on the left. Go through the gates or over the stile if you still have the energy. Follow the marked bridleway diagonally across the large field to a sunken track that drops down and then left by the wall of **Calton Plantations**. Follow the wall leftwards to a gate squeezed between two walled areas of woodland.

Pass through the gate, turn right and follow the wall next to the wood. In the corner of the field a gate with a warning sign to cyclists gives access to a narrow track. Ride down the track past **Calton Houses** and down and round the double bend to a wide straight gravel track. Follow this fast track leftwards to, and through, the carpark at **Calton Lees** where a tea and ice-cream van is usually in residence if you can tolerate the crowds.

Turn left on the B6012, cross the cattle grid, and cycle up the hill through **Chatsworth Park**. Stay on the tarmac as it crests a small ridge and starts to descend. On the right-hand bend leave the road to find, on the left, a grassy terrace that contours round the wooded hillside. This ends at the gates to **Edensor** (pronounced 'Enzer'). Enter the walled village. Ride towards the church, then keep it on your left as you ride up between the remarkably quaint houses. Soon the tarmac becomes a gravel track which is followed straight on, ignoring a track on the right. This long, steady climb meets tarmac again just before a steep, but mercifully short, hill. Turn left and climb the hill.

600 metres after the steep hill, at a point approximately 22.7 km from the start and just before a right-hand bend in the road, turn left through a narrow gap over a broken wall at the edge of woodland. The bridleway is signposted, but the sign is not easily visible from the road unless you have already found the gap! Now enjoy an interesting descent into the Wye Valley by following an obvious path down through woodland, dealing expertly with the mud, ruts and tree roots as you meet them. Cross a narrow part of the golf course. Carry straight on down to meet tarmac at the bottom. Cross the bridge over the Monsal Trail. Take the first road on the right to return to the carpark where you started your ride.

Wye Valley near Haddon Hall.

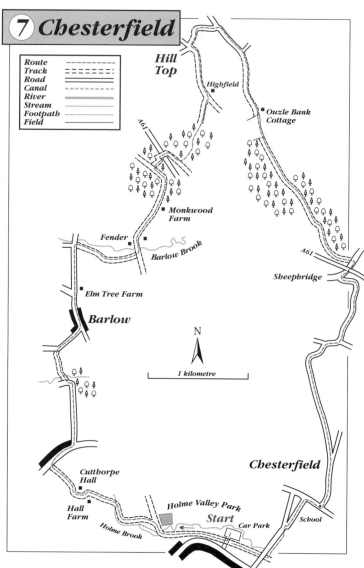

7 Chesterfield

Legend:
- Route
- Track
- Road
- Canal
- River
- Stream
- Footpath
- Field

Hill Top

Highfield

Ouzle Bank Cottage

A61

Monkwood Farm

Fender

Barlow Brook

Elm Tree Farm

Barlow

A61

Sheepbridge

N

1 kilometre

Cutthorpe Hall

Hall Farm

Holme Brook

Holme Valley Park

Start

Car Park

Chesterfield

School

7. Chesterfield

Distance	16 km, 10 miles, 72% off-road.
Time	2 hours.
Map	OS Pathfinder 761 *Chesterfield*.
Facilities	Pubs on route.
Rail Access	Chesterfield Station 3 km from start.

Summary

Emerging from the suburbs of Chesterfield into the hilly countryside around North Derbyshire's chief town, this ride covers surprising terrain and is not without technical interest. It starts with gentle riding through a country park before crossing Linacre Brook and Barlow Brook. It ascends to Highfield and then takes a long and satisfying descent to Sheepbridge. The final 3 km of the ride are mainly on road and cycle-way, but thankfully the roads are not usually busy.

The Route

Start in the **Holme Valley** carpark which is off Linacre Road at OS grid ref. 358726 in the north-western suburbs of **Chesterfield**.

From the carpark ride back out towards the entrance. Just before the entrance, between two speed ramps, a bridleway crosses the carpark approach road. Turn right, west, and ride for approximately 600 metres to a wooden bridge on the right. Cross the bridge over **Holme Brook** to a three-way path junction immediately after the bridge. Go straight on, climbing slightly, beside a low wooden barrier.

Approximately 100 metres from the bridge, go left through a gap in the barrier to enter a path through a narrow strip of scrubby woodland.

Follow this path, going right where it merges with another path. Ride along beside a very small stream to a gravel and pipe crossing point. Immediately after crossing the tiny stream keep left at a fork and follow a muddy path towards **Hall Farm**. At the farm pass to the right of the buildings and go through a gate to a track. Go left, then follow the track rightwards through the farmyard to a short section of tarmac drive. Follow the drive round past **Cutthorpe Hall** and continue along a tree-lined section to the **B6050**.

Turn right and ride for 250 metres before turning left into Common Lane. Follow Common Lane down to a fairly sharp left-hand bend. Just after the bend drop steeply down a path on the right to a ford. Cross the ford and ascend the narrow, grooved path using a surprising measure of technique to overcome what at first do not appear to be obstacles. Follow the path up to meet tarmac.

Go right and up again to a minor road. Turn right and ride down to a T-junction in **Barlow**. Turn left and ride for 250 metres. At a sharp left-hand bend leave the road by going straight on past **Elm Tree Farm**. Follow the road straight on and down to **Lee Bridge**. A few metres before the bridge turn right (opposite a minor road on the left) crossing a cattle grid onto a wide gravel track. Follow this track pleasantly along beside **Barlow Brook** to a road at **Fender**.

Turn left, cross Barlow Brook and follow the road round to the right past a long wooden shed into a tree-lined track, signposted *Monkwood*. Climb steadily past **Monkwood Farm** into the woods. Follow the track to and round a left-hand bend. Approximately 100 metres after the bend, and just before a **Forestry Commission signboard**, turn right and climb a narrow path that ascends to a concrete bridge spanning the **A61**. (This bridge may not be visible from the path junction when the trees are in leaf.) Cross the bridge over a 'river of tortured steel'.

Beyond the bridge a short, fenced path leads to open woodland and a rough junction of paths. Take the path straight on and ride up a few metres to a wider track. Turn right and ride for less than 100 metres to a narrow path on the left that ascends through a very small earth cutting as it leaves the main track.

Ride pleasantly up through woodland to a meeting of paths at the top of the slope. Go right then left to ride up a wooded path between fields on the right and a golf course on the left. This track meets a rough tarmac lane near **Highfield**.

Turn left and ride straight on to a T-junction in a housing estate. Turn right and then immediately right again into Salisbury Road, a wide, rough-surfaced road. Follow this road through a narrower gap to meet tarmac again. Turn right into the first minor road. This road becomes a narrow path and then opens out to a narrow tarmac lane called Links Road. Go straight on to emerge at a minor road. Go right and ride along past **Hallowes Golf Club** into Highgate Lane. At the end of Highgate Lane go right into a broken tarmac lane (ignore Highgate Drive on the left).

Ride down this lane to **Ouzle Bank Cottage**. Go straight on passing through a gate into a field, signposted *Public Bridleway*. Ride down parallel to the left-hand, eastern, boundary of the field. At the far side, go through a bridlegate and follow the muddy track along the lower edge of the wood.

Emerge at a small gorse clearing on the edge of the golf course. Go straight on between low wooden fences to enter another wood. Be careful here; you are crossing a fairway on the golf course. Golfers are driving up from the left.

Carry straight on beside the wood. Caution is required all along this section to avoid low-flying golf balls from golfers who are striving, but unfortunately failing, to achieve accuracy.

Keep going straight on, leaving the golf course and passing to the right of an old chain link fence. Keep going straight on and down into the wood. At a more open area, go straight on and down to a gate near an underpass under the **A61**.

Turn right and go under the A61, signposted *Chesterfield Trading Estate, Sheepbridge*. (**Caution**; just after the bridge watch out for fast traffic coming down the slip road from the A61. Drivers may not see you in the gloom under the bridge.)

Just past the slip road turn left into Sheepbridge Lane. Follow Sheepbridge Lane to a T-junction. Turn right. After 100 metres turn left into Dunstan Lane and follow it to a T-junction by a parade of shops. Turn right and ride to a mini-roundabout where you turn right again, signposted *Barlow*. Just after **Newbold School**, and before the traffic lights, turn left into Newbold Back Lane. After 150 metres,

Hopton Tunnel.

go through a gap on the right onto the signposted cycle-lane that runs alongside the main road. Follow the cycle-lane leftwards and down to an underpass. Go under the underpass and then straight on into **Holmebrook Valley Park** on a bridleway signposted *Cutthorpe*. Ride for 300 metres back to the carpark.

46

Puncture repair in Horseshoe Dale.

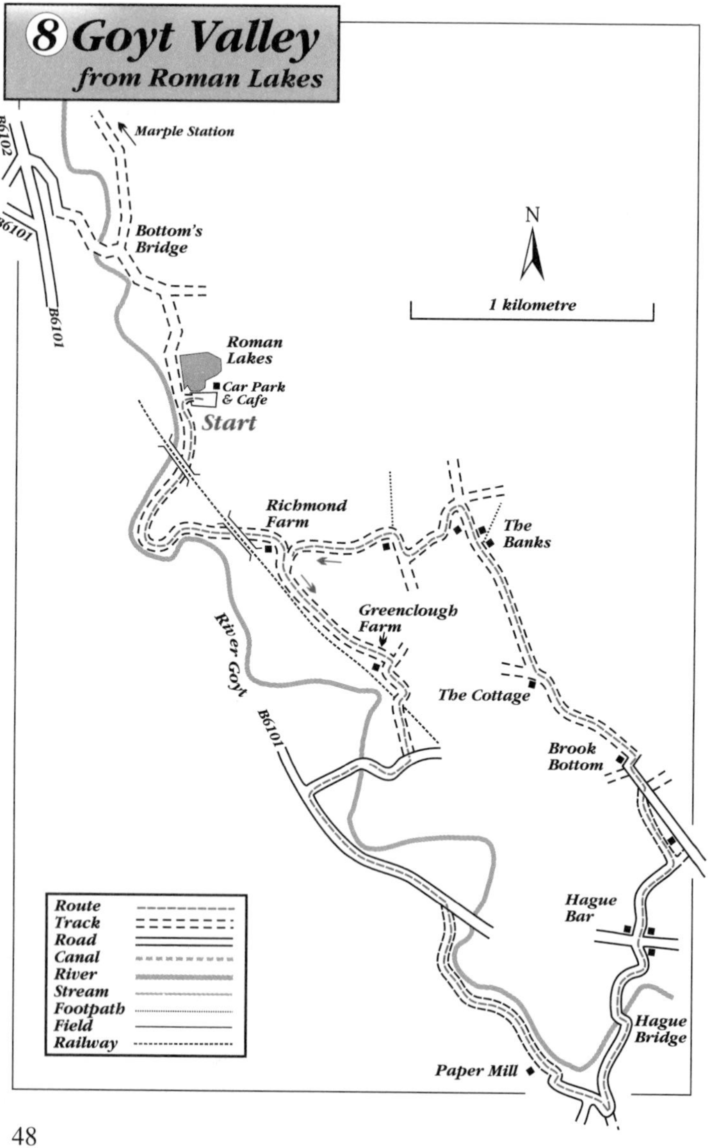

8 Goyt Valley
from Roman Lakes

B6102

B6101

B6101

Marple Station

Bottom's Bridge

Roman Lakes

Car Park & Cafe

Start

N

1 kilometre

Richmond Farm

The Banks

Greenclough Farm

River Goyt

B6101

The Cottage

Brook Bottom

Hague Bar

Hague Bridge

Paper Mill

| Route | Track | Road | Canal | River | Stream | Footpath | Field | Railway |

Route ------
Track ------
Road
Canal
River
Stream
Footpath
Field
Railway ------

8. Goyt Valley from Roman Lakes

Distance	10 km, 6 miles, 75% off-road.
Time	1 hour.
Map	OS Outdoor Leisure 1, *Dark Peak*.
Facilities	Café at start; open every day 8.00 AM to dusk.
Rail Access	Marple Station, 2.3 km from start. Station in Marple Bridge, 1.3 km from start – mainly off-road.

Summary

A very enjoyable, short route that follows the Goyt on pleasant riverside tracks before climbing the steep valley side. It continues by contouring high above the river then descending by path and track back to the start. This route is not quite circular, more lolly-pop shaped! A good introduction for beginners.

The Route

Start at the carpark at the **Roman Lakes Café**, OS grid ref. 969878. This is a privately-owned carpark and permission to use it has been given by the owners of the café, Geraldine and Bernard Sewart.

Leave the carpark by the main gates and turn left onto the broken tarmac track. Ride cheerfully along beside the **River Goyt** passing under a spectacular railway bridge. The first house after the bridge is an old toll house which dates back to the days when this was a major thoroughfare. Follow this easy track through a tunnel under the railway and then past **Richmond Farm**.

Go straight on past the bridleway (the return route) that descends from the left 200 metres after Richmond Farm. Go straight on through a wooded dell ignoring the track that drops back on the right. Pass through a gate to arrive at a track T-junction.

Turn right towards **Greenclough Farm**, then pass through the farmyard going left to pick up a rough tarmac farm track. The track ends at T-junction where the cobbled station approach to **Strines Station** meets a minor road. *(A shorter alternative to the main route can be taken by going left here and then right after the station to join the main route at Brook Bottom. This does not avoid the climb!)*

Assuming you are following the main route go right and ride to the junction with the **B6101**.

Turn left. Ignore the tarmac lane that goes right after 400 metres to **Woodend Farm**. Ride for another 200 metres to **Woodend** – the first cottage on the left. Directly opposite the cottage, and on the right, a tarmac track leaves the road. Immediately to the left of this track is a narrower, wooded path. This is the bridleway.

Follow this gravel path pleasantly beside the River Goyt crossing the **Paper Mill** approach road and continuing to a small carpark by the southern end of the mill. (The OS map is not accurate here as the bridleway has been re-routed.) Turn left and ride up the hill. At the top of the slope go straight on and down into a wooded section. Follow the road round a sharp left-hand bend, over the river and the railway and up to a crossroads.

Go straight across into **Hague Fold Road**. Climb steeply to a point just before a cottage where the road turns left and levels off. Ignore the grassy bridleway that continues straight on. Follow the road to the left in front of the houses. This soon becomes a sandy track that ends at a minor road. Turn left, and ride down to **Brook Bottom**. *(The alternative route joins here.)*

Follow the road right past the Fox Inn and then left to follow the tarmac lane up past Brook Bottom Methodist Church. The tarmac gives way to a stony track.

Follow this track downhill to a point 6.7 km from the start of the ride. On a left-hand bend in the track, a sandy bridleway climbs up to the right opposite a small house on the left. The house has the name *The Cottage* carved on a stone in the small gable end facing the path.

Follow the path to the right. Contour enjoyably along the hillside above the River Goyt ignoring a bridleway signposted to the right

Ostrich Farm near The Banks.

between two houses at **The Banks**. Continue for another 200 metres to a track crossroads. Turn left and follow this fast, rough lane down to a track T-junction. Turn right, signposted *Road Used As Public Path*.

After 100 metres, and just past a house on the left, turn left down a narrow tree-lined path. Despite the dire warnings this is a bridleway. Follow this excellent descent, crossing the fairway of the third hole of Mellor and Townscliffe golf course *en route*. (Look out for small white missiles from your left!) The path ends at a T-junction where you rejoin the outward route.

Turn right and follow the riverside track past **Richmond Farm**, through the tunnel, underneath the arches and so back to the carpark at Roman Lakes for a well-earned visit to the café.

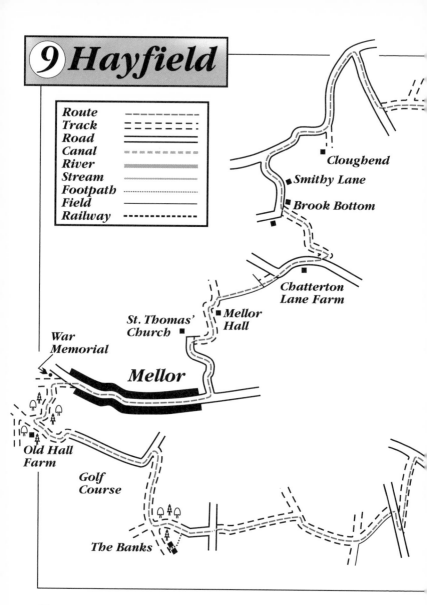

9 Hayfield

Route	-------
Track	= = = =
Road	———
Canal	- - - -
River	=======
Stream	———
Footpath	········
Field	———
Railway	- - - - -

Cloughend

Smithy Lane

Brook Bottom

Chatterton
Lane Farm

St. Thomas'
Church

Mellor
Hall

War
Memorial

Mellor

Old Hall
Farm

Golf
Course

The Banks

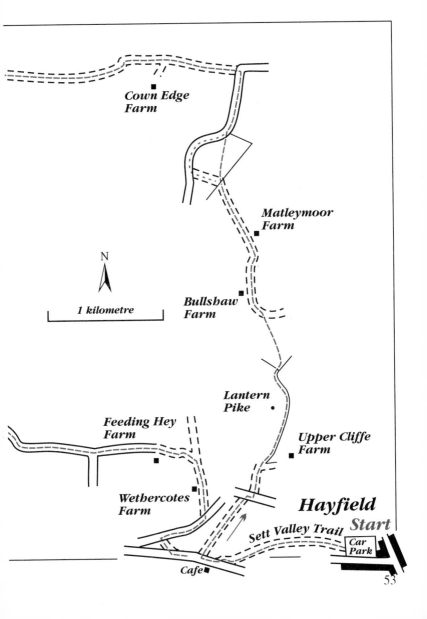

Cown Edge
Farm

Matleymoor
Farm

N

1 kilometre

Bullshaw
Farm

Lantern
Pike

Feeding Hey
Farm

Upper Cliffe
Farm

Wethercotes
Farm

Hayfield
Start

Sett Valley Trail

Car
Park

Cafe

9. Hayfield

Distance	27 km, 17 miles, 76% off-road.
Time	4 hours.
Map	OS Outdoor Leisure 1 *Dark Peak*.
Facilities	Cafés at Spinners Bottom (not always open) and Roman Lakes (always open). Shop at start. Pubs *en route*.
Rail Access	New Mills Station (2.5 km from start mainly off-road).

Summary
A satisfying ride that combines high moorland with the more subtle delights of the lower Goyt Valley. It crosses some quite strenuous terrain and a couple of short sections will defeat all but the most able riders. The ride starts low in the Sett Valley, climbs out via Lantern Pike and circles round to descend into the Goyt Valley. The long climb over Cobden Edge leads to a descent and a further climb to Wethercotes. A descent back into the Sett Valley is followed by re-riding a short section of the Sett Valley Trail back to Hayfield.

The Route
Start from the Sett Valley Trail carpark in **Hayfield** at OS grid ref. 036869. Ride through the carpark to the start of the Trail. Follow the trail for 1.5 km to a road. Just before the road the trail drops down a short incline on the right, to a gate. Go through the gate and turn right on the road – noting the café on your left for the return journey. Ride down the hill for 200 metres, crossing the River Sett, to a terrace of stone houses on the right. At the end of the terrace, take the cobbled and signposted bridleway to the right.

Ride up over small, loose boulders; this is tricky at first but it soon eases. At the top go through a gate to a junction with a tarmac track.

Go left, uphill, to a road. Turn right and then almost immediately left up a tarmac-surfaced bridleway which is ascended to a path junction by **Upper Cliffe Farm**. Go straight on and climb towards **Lantern Pike** on the rutted path beside the wall. You will be doing well if you complete this section without putting a foot down!

Eventually the bridleway descends a short, loose slope to a gate. Go through the gate, carry straight on for 20 metres and then turn left, heading down the large field towards a green signpost which is just visible on the far (northern) wall of the field. The bridleway is not well-marked here; spot the green signpost, look at your map and take the best line you can.

When you reach the signpost go through a gate to join a gravel track at a bend. Go straight on, signposted *Matley Moor*. Follow this track, ignoring the entrance to **Bullshaw Farm** on the left. Pass to the left of **Matleymoor Farm** and follow the walled bridleway through a gate to a more open field. Carry straight on passing through a small cutting and another gate to the start of a broad track that descends to a road.

Just after this gate, a solitary stone gatepost can be seen in the wall on the right. The bridleway crosses the wall by the gatepost and then cuts diagonally across the hillside on a sheep track to the bend in the road. (This is the more interesting route, but the lift over the wall can be avoided by riding straight on down the track to the road and turning right to reach the bend.)

Whichever route you choose, you will arrive at the bend in the road where the bridleway emerges from the field. Go north-north-east along the road for approximately 500 metres to a sharp right-hand bend. Turn left on the farm approach road and pass through the gate, signposted *Cown Edge Farm.*

Ride for approximately 700 metres to a left-hand bend. Leave the farm track here for the rough, sunken bridleway that carries straight on. Climb the track to the crest of **Cown Edge** where – if you are lucky – a thought-provoking view awaits.

Follow the track downhill and through a gate. After the gate turn left and, after a few metres, right. This narrower path leads down to a wider sandy track. Go straight on down this fast track to join another track. Go left and ride for 100 metres to a road. Turn right and after 400 metres turn left at a T-junction. Ride over the hill, ignore a tempting looking track to the left, then turn left into **Smithy Lane** – a named tarmac minor road approximately 11 km from the start.

Ride down Smithy Lane through **Brook Bottom**. Just after crossing the brook turn left into a rough and stony track. Follow this, crossing a small ford, then round a sharp right-hand bend to meet a minor road.

Turn right and ride through **Chatterton Lane Farm** to a sharp right-hand bend approximately 12.6 km from the start of the ride. Go straight on, following a signposted gravel track. Carry straight on through a gate, crossing a field to join a tarmac drive. Go leftwards up the drive towards **Mellor Hall**. Follow the signposted bridleway passing to the right of the Hall. Pass through a small paved yard in front of a converted barn and through one of a pair of ornate wood and metal gates.

Carry on along the rough tarmac to **St. Thomas' Church**. Turn left and ride down towards **Mellor** village. At the T-junction turn right.

Ride through the village to a point where the main road makes a right-hand bend by a **war memorial**, 1.4 km from the T-junction. Leave the road here by following the wide gravel road straight on in the same direction you have been travelling.

After a few metres turn left into **Old Hall Lane**. This bone-shattering descent ends at a track T-junction by a unique culvert with ornate stone portals near **Old Hall Farm**. (*If you would like to visit the café at Roman Lakes, go right then take the next track left to find the café in a carpark just past the lake on the left. See Goyt Valley route for more detail.*)

Turn left and ascend the track. Carry straight on, over tarmac, signposted *Mellor, Cobden Edge*. Pass through the grounds of **Mellor and Townscliffe Golf Club**, climbing round a left-hand-bend to take the next road on the right that ascends through the golf course. This junction is marked by a low dry-stone wall and small notice warning of low-flying golf balls.

Follow this broken tarmac track as it contours along Cobden Edge. The tarmac track ends at a path junction where a track drops down to the right and another goes straight on, climbing gently. A third track ascends steeply leftwards through a concealing holly bush.

Take this third track and climb with difficulty to an open area and path junction. Go left and up an even more testing section to meet a gravel track ascending from the right. Go straight on, still climbing but now on tarmac, past a farm entrance to a T-junction with another minor road. Go straight across and ascend the rough track to the crest of the ridge.

Follow this track (Black Lane) to a T-junction with another track. Turn right and pick your way along **Primrose Lane** to a track crossroads. Go straight across and descend to a road.

Turn right and ride for 100 metres to turn left into an inviting track which cuts back left and descends northwards. At the end of this fun descent turn right on the road. Ride steeply down and then up to a junction on a right-hand bend. Turn left to climb the lane, curiously signposted *Prohibition Of Driving*.

Ride up past **Feeding Hey Farm**, straight on through the gate and up the narrower path. At the top pass through a gate, ride up for a few metres and turn right at a track T-junction.

Ride down through **Wethercotes Farm** to a T-junction with a minor road overlooking the valley.

Turn right and ride for 400 metres to a signposted bridleway which is on the left just after a right-hand bend and a short steep descent. (Look out for the end of a wooden fence on the left that surrounds a small quarry.) This turning is easy to miss.

Go down the narrow path – a steep descent – to **Spinner Bottom**. Turn left and ride down to meet the outward route on the **River Sett** near the café. Turn left through the gate just after the entrance to an industrial estate and ride up a path beside the road to rejoin the **Sett Valley Trail**.

Turn left at the top and retrace your outward route along the Trail to the start and finish of the ride.

Taking a tumble in Broad Clough.

Harden Hill Road.

10 Holmbridge & Digley

Legend:
- Route
- Track
- Road
- Canal
- River
- Stream
- Footpath
- Field
- Railway

Green Bottom
Royd Bridge
Ash Royd
Magdalen Road
Harden Moss Road
Harden Hill Road
A635
A635
Goodbent Lodge
Marsden Clough
Digley Reservoir
Holmbridge
A6024
A6024
Car Park
Start
Holme
A6024
Rake Dike
A6024
Ramsden Reservoir
Ramsden Road
White Gate Road
Riding Wood Reservoir
Yatebolme Reservoir

N

1 kilometre

10. Holmbridge & Digley

Distance	24 km, 15 miles, 61% off-road.
Time	3 hours.
Map	OS Outdoor Leisure 1 *Dark Peak*. (This route does not appear on the older versions of the Dark Peak map.)
Facilities	Pubs in Holme and Holmbridge.
Rail Access	Not practical.

Summary

A very enjoyable route amongst the open hills, sheltered woodlands and reservoirs above Holmbridge on the north-eastern edge of the Peak District. It consists of two good, long sections of off-road linked by quite a long section of tarmac. The final section of track above Marsden Clough is particularly good. A good route for parties of very mixed ability and ambition as it can easily be split (*marked in text*) just after Holmbridge with the second big climb still to come.

The Route

Park at a small carpark on the Holme to Digley Reservoir road, OS grid ref. 109067.

Leave the carpark and turn right to ride up the road towards Holme. Where the minor road joins the **A6024** in the centre of **Holme**, turn right. Follow the main road for about 1 km. The road descends, crosses **Rake Dike** at a left-hand bend and then ascends to a sharp right-hand bend. Leave the road here by taking the obvious wide track straight on.

Follow this track, ignoring another that joins from the right after 400 metres. The track now skirts the edge of woodland, descends into **Netherley Clough**, passes under the dam wall of **Yateholme Reservoir** and then runs through woodland to cross the dam wall of **Riding Wood Reservoir**.

On leaving the dam follow the track left and then after 100 metres, directly opposite a house, turn right up a steep, signposted bridleway.

Next comes the ascent of **Ramsden Edge**; a steady climb of 120 metres vertical interval. Follow the track round a sharp left-hand bend. Curve right at the next 'junction' and then up again to a sharp left-hand bend where a track joins from the right. Follow the track left, still climbing, to a curving right-hand bend where at last it begins to level off. Follow **Ramsden Road** to a minor road.

Go straight across onto the wide gravel road (**White Gate Road**) and ride for 1 km to where the track becomes tarmac by **Moorfield Farm**. Carry on for another 250 metres to where a walled, sandy track leaves the road on the left. Follow this track over the crest of the ridge and down past a quarry entrance to a short descent that ends at a minor road at **Upper Woodhouse**. Go straight across the first road and descend a very short continuation track to a second, lower road.

Turn right and descend into Holmbridge round sharp bends, ignoring all left turnings for nearly 1 km until reaching Dobb Top Road on the left. Turn left into Dobb Top Road and follow it down to the A6024 in **Holmbridge**.

Turn right and cross the River Holme. Curve right past the Church and then, just past the Post Office and before the Bridge Tavern, turn left up a steep lane. Ignore the first minor road on the right. Ride on leaving the houses behind to turn right 500 metres from the Bridge Tavern. *(Straight on here, then left over the dam wall will take you back to the start.)*

After another 500 metres go left and, at the crossroads, go right into Green Gate Road. Follow this up to a crossroads with the A635. Turn left and ride for 400 metres to a bridleway on the right.

Follow this track as it skirts **Harden Hill** and then enjoy a long descent to **Royd Bridge**.

Turn left and follow the minor road past Green Bottom and up to a sharp right-hand bend. From here there are two alternatives:

Alternative 1, ***Harden Moss Road***. Go straight on up the rough tarmac track. Follow it through a muddy dip and up to the main **A635**. Turn right and ride for 800 metres to find, on the left, a

Springs Road.

signposted bridleway that leaves the road through a wooden gate. This alternative is easier, but involves more road riding.

Alternative 2, *Magdalen Road*. Follow the tarmac lane right. Go round a left-hand bend and pass the entrance to **Ash Royd**. Go straight on into a field and continue straight on over tussocks and grooved paths. Follow this tiring terrain to a wider track. Go straight on to meet the **A635**. Turn right. After 100 metres you will find, on the left, a signposted bridleway that leaves the road through a wooden gate. This alternative is harder, but gives less road riding.

Continuation of both routes: Go left down the track (**Springs Road**) which winds through numerous walls and is part paved with grooved gritstone slabs; a remnant of its former glory. Turn sharp left where a high wall and 'ladder' stile appears to bar the way on.

Descend the wide and fast **Nether Lane** passing a few isolated farms. The track ends all too soon at a minor road. Go right. Turn right at the crossroads. Negotiate sharp bends and then turn right to cross the dam wall of **Digley Reservoir** back to the carpark.

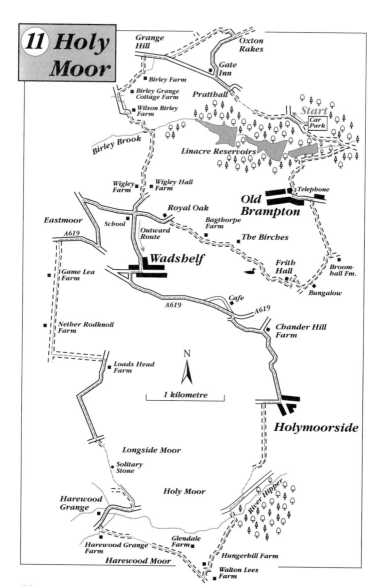

11 Holy Moor

Grange Hill

Oxton Rakes

Gate Inn

Pratthall

■ Birley Farm

■ Birley Grange Cottage Farm

■ Wilson Birley Farm

Start
Car Park

Birley Brook

Linacre Reservoirs

Wigley Farm ■   ■ Wigley Hall Farm

Telephone

Old Brampton

Royal Oak

Eastmoor

School

Bagthorpe Farm

A619

Outward Route

Wadshelf

■ The Birches

Frith Hall

Broomball Fm.

■ Game Lea Farm

A619

Cafe

A619

Bungalow

■ Nether Rodknoll Farm

■ Chander Hill Farm

N

1 kilometre

■ Loads Head Farm

Holymoorside

Longside Moor

• Solitary Stone

Holy Moor

River Hipper

Harewood Grange

■ Harewood Grange Farm

■ Glendale Farm

■ Hungerbill Farm

Harewood Moor

■ Walton Lees Farm

11. Holy Moor

Distance	26 km, 16 miles, 65% off-road.
Time	3.5 hours.
Map	OS Outdoor Leisure 24 *White Peak*.
Facilities	Pubs and a lay-by snack-bar.
Rail Access	Not practical.

Summary
This enjoyable and interesting 'figure-of-eight' ride explores the farm, wood and open moorland between Chesterfield and Baslow. Some sections can be vexingly glutinous after rain but these are quite short and balanced by Sahara-like sections that seem to stay dry in all conditions. The ride starts near Linacre Reservoirs, circles north via Oxton Rake before cutting back south to circumnavigate Holy Moor. A long section of good farm track brings you back to Old Brampton and the delightful ride past the lower reservoir to finish.

This route is another good choice for a mixed ability party as the ride can be conveniently split at Wigley Primary School with the serious team and the pub team meeting at The Royal Oak to ride the last section together.

The Route
Start from the Linacre Reservoirs carpark at OS grid ref. 336727. Ride back along the carpark approach road towards the main road. Where the approach road makes a sharp right-hand turn, take the track on the left that skirts the northern edge of a wood.

At the end of the wood cross into a field and follow the path straight across to enter a walled track. This track meets the road at **Pratthall**. Turn left and follow the road for 200 metres to the first road on the right, next to the **Gate Inn** and signposted *Oxton Rakes*.

Follow the road down and then round a sharp left-hand bend, ignoring the tempting, wide, grassy track straight on; it is a footpath. After a few metres go round another left-hand bend to the start of a bridleway on the right.

Ascend the bridleway, ignoring another bridleway on the right. It is a long and steady climb, apart from one particularly muddy dip, before meeting the B6050 below the summit of **Grange Hill**. Turn right and ride up for 150 metres, passing a minor road on the right and a footpath on the left. Take the farm entrance on the left just before a left-hand bend road sign. This entrance can also be identified by two round stone pillars with the sign *Birley Grange Farm, Private Road, Footpath Only*. Despite the sign this is a bridleway. Follow the track down past the entrance to **Birley Farm** and **Birley Grange Cottage Farm**. Take the bridleway straight on, keeping a small pond and the power line on your left. Bypass the wooden gate to join a tarmac farm road. Turn left, cross a small ford and follow the road for a couple of hundred metres to just before the imposing gates of **Wilson Birley Farm**. Go through a bridlegate on the left. Cross the field towards the farm, rejoining the road for the last few metres to reach the farm entrance. **<u>Do not enter the farmyard</u>**.

Go over the cattle grid and straight on down the grassy walled track. This becomes narrower and muddy as it descends to the valley floor. At the bottom pass through a gate and follow the path leftwards beside a small stream. After a few metres the path passes through the remains of a stone gateway then turns right and begins to climb beside another stream in a small valley. Follow this path up through woodland to a junction with a footpath joining from the left by a wooden branch fence. Follow the narrow path to the right to reach tarmac at **Wigley Farm**. Turn right and follow the tarmac farm track out to meet a minor road at a crossroads with **Wigley Primary School** opposite.

Cross over into School Lane and follow it into the village of **Wadshelf**. In Wadshelf follow the road sharp right, then take the next road left, Bradshaw Lane, to meet the A619. Turn left and ride along this busy main road for 1.5 km. Just past a large lay-by (where, with luck, the snack-bar will be open) take a minor road on the right, signposted *Holymoorside*. Follow this road, at first round to the left and then, after 500 metres, right, past **Chander Hill Farm**. Follow the road down to a crossroads on the outskirts of **Holymoorside**.

Turn right. Ride up the hill for 150 metres to the start of a bridleway on the left. A faded wooden fingerpost reads *Hungerhill Lane*. Ride up the sandy track to the rim of the **River Hipper** valley. A good place for lunch!

Follow the path to the right, contouring round the upper edge of the valley for 150 metres, until the obvious path starts to descend diagonally down the steep hillside. An excellent, narrow descent leads to a minor road. Turn right and ride for 300 metres, ignoring a footpath on the left which is marked by two stone pillars. The bridleway leaves the road on the left just before a right-hand bend. Continue the descent into the valley bottom, crossing the river to continue up the tree-lined and walled path round bends and over rocky steps. The path meets a gravel track. Carry straight on along the track past **Hungerhill Farm** to a junction of bridleways near **Walton Lees Farm**.

Turn sharp right following the signposted bridleway north-west. Pass the entrance to **Glendale Farm**, then go through a double wooden gate and out across the open moor. Contour across the sloping moor on a good path that snakes through the heather. On the far side of the moor the path meets the corner of a stone-walled field. Pass to the left of the corner. Carry straight on through another double gate by **Harewood Grange Farm** and follow the gravel track rightwards and up to the road.

Turn right and follow the road for 600 metres to a signposted bridleway on the left. Pass through the gate to climb straight up the hillside next to the wall. (At this point, which is about as far from the start as you can get, you may hear a depressing metallic crack as your chain ring disintegrates. Mine did; but luckily I had top gear for the rest of the ride.)

Ignore the first grassy track on the left, but follow the path as it curves left below the steep crest of the ridge. Follow the track up to a break of slope where the moorland gives way to open grass without a fence or wall. *(In poor visibility you may need to use your map and compass for the next section. A bearing of 334 degrees magnetic will take you to the T-junction.)* In good visibility, head straight across the field to a small, solitary stone. From the stone, a gate by a tree is visible on the horizon in roughly the same direction as you have been riding. Head for this. The bridleway ends at the gate on a T-junction of minor roads.

Go straight across and follow the road for 1.1 km until, just past **Loads Head Farm**, a straight track leaves the road on the left. The track leads to a junction. Turn right and ride dead straight downhill for 1.4 km on a very good surface to meet the A619 at **Eastmoor**. Watch out for ruts near the farm entrance.

Turn right and take the first tarmac road on the left, signposted *Cutthorpe*. Take the next road on the right. Go straight across the crossroads to reach the **Royal Oak**. Opposite the Royal Oak take the tarmac minor road to the right. This soon becomes a gravel track. Pass **Bagthorpe Farm** by going straight on and bypassing the metal gate by a squeeze on its left. Follow the bridleway between hedges to a right turn by the entrance to **The Birches**. Drop down the walled bridleway passing a duck pond and through the farmyard of **Frith Hall**. Climb up to a track T-junction. Turn left passing a bungalow.

Ride down the track. Just before **Broomhall Farm** turn left into a wide, tree-lined bridleway. This junction is marked by a distinctive, low brick wall with rounded stone capping. Ride up to meet the road in **Old Brampton**. Turn left. Follow the road for 300 metres to a bridleway on the right with a telephone box on the corner. This enjoyable descent takes you past the lower **Linacre Reservoir** and down to a stone bridge in a beech wood. Turn left, cross the bridge and climb up to the carpark where you began your ride.

Gunthwaite Lane. (opp.)

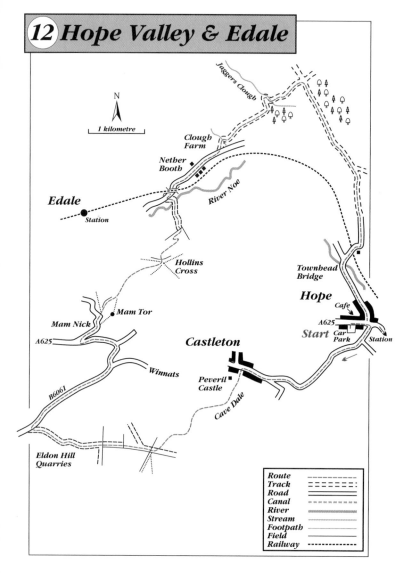

12 Hope Valley & Edale

N

1 kilometre

Joggers Clough

Clough Farm

Nether Booth

Edale

Station

River Noe

Hollins Cross

Townhead Bridge

Mam Tor

Hope

Cafe

Mam Nick

A625

A625

Start

Car Park

Station

Castleton

B6061

Winnats

Peveril Castle

Cave Dale

Eldon Hill Quarries

Route	
Track	-------
Road	————
Canal	—·—·—·
River	～～～
Stream	
Footpath	·········
Field	
Railway	--------

12. Hope Valley and Edale

Distance	23 km, 14 miles, 78% off-road.
Time	3 hours.
Maps	OS Outdoor Leisure 1 *Dark Peak*.
Facilities	The Woodbine Café in Hope is one of the Peak's best cafés. Not only do they serve the best and biggest mugs of tea and superb home-made cakes and pies, they also sell a few bike spares!
Rail Access	Hope Station (1 km from start).

Summary

A very satisfying ride crossing both high limestone and gritstone country. The ascent of Cave Dale is long and rocky; some carrying will almost certainly be necessary in the middle part. The route then crosses the limestone plateau, skirts the summit of Mam Tor, descends the ridge to Hollins Cross and continues down into the Edale valley. A long, but reasonable, climb ascends to Hope Brink. An excellent descent returns to Hope.

The Route

Start at the carpark in **Hope**, opposite the Woodbine Café, at OS grid ref. 172835. Turn right, east, on the A625. After a few metres turn right just past the Woodroffe Arms Hotel into Pindale Road. Follow this minor road past the Hope Valley Cement Works and then on, round the double bend, towards Castleton. Follow the road over and down, keeping right when a road joins from the left, to the outskirts of **Castleton**. Take the first narrow tarmac lane to the left, just before Cave Dale Cottage. A wooden fingerpost on the opposite side of the road indicates the *Limestone Way*.

Ride up through the narrow cleft into **Cave Dale**. Continue straight on up the dale: the rocky and rubble parts are probably not rideable.

At the top the dale opens out and becomes a small, grassy valley. Follow the valley straight on and eventually curve slightly left following a wall to reach double wooden gates and a track at a point 5.1 km from the start of the ride.

Turn right, pass through a gate and follow the track. After 200 metres a track forks off to the right. Carry straight on alongside a wall on the left. At the end of the field go straight on through a gate and down a long, fast track that passes beside **Eldon Hill Quarry**. At the bottom turn right on the **B6061**. After 1.8 km follow the B6061 round to the left, signposted *Chapel-en-le-Frith*, (the road to the right drops down Winnats Pass to Castleton). After 400 metres turn left again to join the **A625**, signposted *Chapel-en-le-Frith, Edale, Rushup*. Ride along the A625 for 600 metres to take the first turning on the right, just past the carpark and signposted *Barber Booth, Edale*.

Ride steeply up to **Mam Nick** and descend a few metres down the Edale side. On the right, at the far end of a lay-by, take the bridleway that contours round below the summit of Mam Tor. Follow the rutted path round to the crest of the ridge and descend to **Hollins Cross**, the lowest point on the Mam Tor – Lose Hill ridge which is marked by a circular stone memorial. There are stunning views from everywhere along this ridge and it is one of Derbyshire's premier hang-gliding and paragliding sites. Stay clear of launching and landing flyers who may be crossing your path.

Leave the ridge at Hollins Cross by descending to the left. There are two bridleways that go left. The one you want passes through a gap in a low, ruined wall and is the right-hand (more easterly) of the pair.

Follow this testing path diagonally down, through a sharp left and then right-hand bend, to a gate in the angle formed by two walls. Go through the gate and continue down past **Backtor Farm**. At the bottom go left over a small bridge over the **River Noe** and up to the minor road.

Turn right and ride for 1.2 km to a point 15.3 km from the start of the ride where a bridleway climbs away from the road to the left.

Cave Dale.

Nearby, a 1905 vintage signpost, obviously erected in a more verbose age, reads *Public Footpath and Bridleroad to Alport, Ashopton, Derwent, Snake Inn and Glossop.*

Follow this pleasant track up to **Clough Farm**. Cross a small ford by the farm and go through a gate beyond. Take the wide gravel path straight on that ascends and then curves round to the left. Avoid the track that drops down right to the valley floor. A long steady climb ends with a descent round sharp bends into **Jaggers Clough**. Cross the wide ford and climb, steeply at first, all the way to the crest of the ridge.

Turn right, signposted *Winhill and Hope*, and descend along the spine of the ridge. After the second gate, 18.6 km from the start, follow the sunken track straight on, avoiding the track that ascends to the left.

Follow this good path, which at first contours across the face of **Hope Brink**, before enjoying a long and fast descent into the valley. Pass round to the right by **Fullwood Stile Farm** and continue the descent to meet the minor road at **Townhead Bridge**. Turn left, cross the bridge, and follow the road to a T-junction in **Hope**. Turn right and ride back past the Woodroffe Arms Hotel to the carpark.

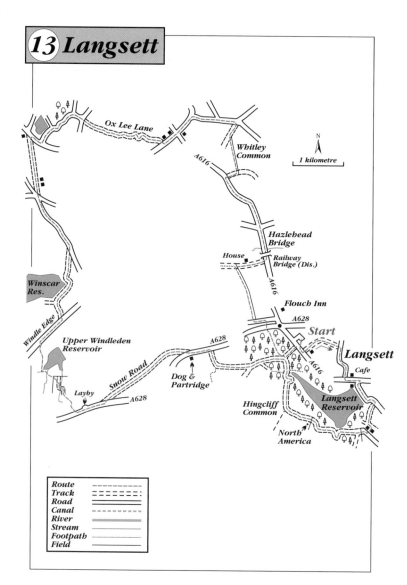

13 Langsett

Ox Lee Lane

Whitley Common

A616

N

1 kilometre

Hazlehead Bridge

House

Railway Bridge (Dis.)

A616

Winscar Res.

Flouch Inn

A628

Start

Windle Edge

Upper Windleden Reservoir

A628

Langsett

Snow Road

Dog & Partridge

A628

Layby

Cafe

A616

Hingcliff Common

Langsett Reservoir

North America

Route	------
Track	= = = =
Road	————
Canal	— — —
River	
Stream	
Footpath	········
Field	

13. Langsett

Distance	31 km, 19 miles, 69% off-road.
Time	4.5 hours.
Map	OS Outdoor Leisure 1 *Dark Peak*.
Facilities	Café and pub in Langsett.
Rail Access	Penistone Station (6 km from start, about 50% off-road).

Summary
A fine, challenging ride through the hills on the extreme northern edge of the Peak District. It covers a wide and interesting variety of rideable terrain, crossing everything from forest tracks and paths to open moorland and old drovers roads. Except for the café in Langsett, there are no shops, few pubs and parts of the ride are quite isolated and exposed – reaching over 450 metres ASL at one point – so appropriate clothing and sufficient food and liquid are essential.

The Route
Start from the Langsett (Flouch) carpark which will be found at grid ref. 201011, approximately 200 metres south-west of the new roundabout at the A628/A616 junction. (The newly-built section of the A628 and the roundabout are not shown on older Dark Peak maps.) This carpark is 1.5 kilometres north-west of the tiny village of Langsett and should not be confused with the other Langsett carpark which is nearer the village and on the south-west side of the road.

Leave the carpark via a path near the information board, passing through a gate onto the **A616**. Turn left and ride for 200 metres to a signposted bridleway on the left.

Follow the bridleway, which is tarmacked for the first few metres, up the hillside past the farm. Follow the broad, grassy track to a minor road. Turn right and descend to join the A616 in **Langsett**.

Turn left and ride with care for 150 metres along this fast and busy road to a minor road on the right just past the **Waggon & Horses**, signposted *Strines, Derwent Valley*.

Follow the road across the dam that retains Langsett Reservoir. On leaving the dam the road curves first left and then to the right. After the right-hand bend and at the end of a small wood, turn right into a track, signposted *Public Bridleway*. Follow this surfaced track, keeping left where a narrower path forks to the right. The track ends at **Upper Midhope** where it meets a concrete lane with houses opposite.

Turn left and then immediately right between two houses to take a narrower path that curves to the right behind the houses. At the bottom of this short descent go right, pass through a gap beside a barrier and ride down the concrete road, signposted *Privilege Footpath*. Pass through a gate and go straight on down into the wood on a track. The track descends and crosses a small bridge, then climbs steadily all the way to **North America**.

Go straight on passing the ruins of an old farm named after the destination of the last inhabitants who emigrated from here in the 1930s. Beyond the ruins go straight on across the open moor following a well-defined path. Ascend to a path junction at **Hingcliff Common**. This junction is marked by a tumbledown wall and two stone pillars

Turn right and descend this rocky track, skirting the edge of a forest and curving round to a gate and bridge across the **Little Don River**. Cross the river, ascend the short steep bank, and at the top go left climbing gently into **Crookland Wood**.

After 250 metres – where the track you are following curves rightwards – descend a bank on the left, then go left again following the track that descends between two dry-stone walls. (Be careful not to take the narrower path to the left that crosses the stream – this is the return route.) Follow the track as it skirts the edge of coniferous woodland. At the far side of the wood bear right onto another track that merges from the left. After 250 metres go right again passing through a gate into a walled track, signposted *Bord Hill*. Go straight on over a farm access track and follow the track to its end at a gate. Go through the gate and turn right. Follow the path out to meet the **A628**.

Turn left and ride beside this busy road for 500 metres. On the left-hand bend about 50 metres past the **Dog & Partridge** a bridleway leaves the road on the right, heading in a westerly direction. Cross the road and enter **Snow Road** – a track. It is a steady climb of nearly 2 km to a gap in the snow fences and the A628 road.

Turn right. (Although it is probably not strictly legal it is much safer to stay on the same side of the road and ride on the grass verge rather than to ride on the road and therefore have to cross the road – and the high speed traffic – twice. A case for cycle lanes if ever there was one!)

Ride along the A628 for approximately 400 metres to a lay-by on the right. Some 300 metres after the lay-by leave the road by taking the signposted bridleway on the right. This path is very boggy at first but soon improves as it contours round **South Nab** – a small hill. Follow this path in a north-westerly direction as it descends towards a stream in a small but deep valley. The path follows the true right bank of the stream before crossing the stream via a stone bridge.

Follow the left bank for only 50 metres to a lone tree on the right of the path. Leave the main path here climbing diagonally up the bank on the left. At first the path is not clearly defined, but it becomes clearer as you continue in roughly the same direction towards a gate in the corner of the field approximately 100 metres from the lone tree.

Go through the gate and follow the path straight on into a larger valley. The path descends steeply to a small wooden bridge. On the far side of the bridge, the path climbs round a shoulder and then descends to cross another small stream at the western end of **Upper Windleden Reservoir**.

The path now ascends in a northerly direction to a minor road on **Windle Edge**. Turn right and follow the road for 600 metres to a left turn into a carpark at **Winscar Reservoir**. Follow the tarmac across the dam wall and climb to a minor road on the far side. Turn left and ride up and over the crest of the hill. Descend to a crossroads. Go straight across into a broad gravel track. Go down this track – a fast, bumpy ride – to another crossroads. Turn right and ride for 500 metres to turn left into Strines Moor Road. Ride past a reservoir. At the fork in the road go right. At another fork in the road go right again. Ride to a T-junction.

Go straight across into a track, named *Ox Lee Lane*. Carry straight on, always following the sunken or walled track of this old drovers way to **Ox Lee**, a ruined farm. Go straight on, crossing a ruined wall to ascend into a narrow groove. Follow the track up and to the right. Where it opens out, go left through a gate to climb the hillside towards two wooden pylons carrying power lines. At the top, pass through a gate and follow the track round to the right, crossing fields, to a minor road.

Turn left and ride to a crossroads. Go straight across and ride up to Lower Maythorn Lane on the right. Turn right and follow the Lower Maythorn Lane for approximately 900 metres to a junction on a gentle right-hand bend.

A bridleway leaves the road on the right. Follow this rough track for 300 metres then go left into a field. Follow the left (east) boundary of the field over the crest of a hill and down to a track. Turn right and go along the track to the **A616** road.

Turn left and ride along the road for approximately 1.8 km passing over a crossroads and descending to **Hazlehead Bridge**. Approximately 100 metres after the bridge and just after an old railway bridge over the road, turn right into a tarmac lane. Follow this lane straight on to a house.

The bridleway goes straight on, appearing to go through the garden of the house. Please keep disturbance to a minimum through this section. Keep the house – and the lawn beyond – on your right, and continue straight on ascending a narrower path at the far end of the garden.

Broad Clough.

After this short climb go through a gate and then immediately left through another gate into a field. Follow the left (east) wall of the field beside a deep ditch for 1.3 km to Old Manchester Road.

Turn left and ride for 200 metres to where the road passes through a gap in a newly built dry-stone wall. Turn right on the signposted bridleway that leaves the road through a gap in the boundary wall next to a stile and skirts the edge of a wood next to a wall.

Cross straight over the newly built section of the **A628** (not marked on older Dark Peak maps). Follow the bridleway straight on into the woods. Go straight on across a firebreak where power lines cross your route. Descend through the plantation to a more open area. Follow the path round to the left to return to the junction of bridleways you passed on the outwards route.

Go left along the broad track and follow it to the **A616**. Go straight across to follow the short path back to the carpark.

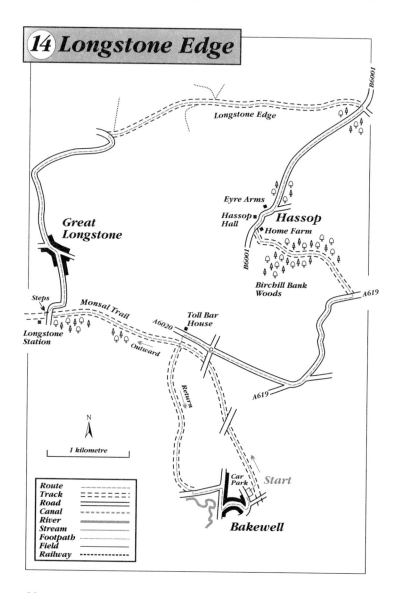

14 Longstone Edge

Longstone Edge

B6001

Great
Longstone

Eyre Arms

Hassop
Hall

Hassop

Home Farm

Birchill Bank
Woods

A619

Steps

Monsal Trail

Toll Bar
House

A6020

Longstone
Station

Outward

B6001

Return

A619

N

1 kilometre

Car
Park

Start

Route
Track
Road
Canal
River
Stream
Footpath
Field
Railway

Bakewell

14. Longstone Edge

Distance	20 km, 12 miles, 60% off-road.
Time	2 hours.
Map	OS Outdoor Leisure 24 *White Peak*.
Facilities	Pubs and cafés in Bakewell, Great Longstone and Hassop.
Rail Access	Not practical.

Summary

Another excellent figure-of-eight ride in the central Peak. It starts at the disused Bakewell Station and follows the Monsal Trail before climbing Longstone Edge. A long, fast descent and a road leads via Hassop to a ford and a forest bridleway. The route crosses the Monsal Trail and ends with a descent to Bakewell. This is a good poor weather route: the higher part of the route is fast and well-surfaced with easy navigation, and the muddy sections are short.

The Route

Start at the Monsal Trail carpark by the disused Bakewell Station at OS grid ref. 222690. (See Chatsworth West ride for directions to carpark). Exit from the carpark to the left of the old station buildings and turn left, north, along the **Monsal Trail**. Trundle along the trail for 3.7 km, passing under five bridges, to **Longstone Station**. Leave the Trail here by climbing the short set of steps on the right just after passing under a bridge. At the top of the steps turn left and ride along the road into **Great Longstone**. Turn left at a T-junction by an old stone pillar set on a triangle of grass. Follow this road to a right turn into Moor Road by an old water pump and stone trough, signposted *Longstone Edge*.

Ride up to **Longstone Edge**, climbing steeply at first and then more gently. At the summit, 6.6 km from the start of the ride, the road makes a sharp left turn. Leave the road by the wide gravel track on the right that crosses a cattle grid and ascends eastwards. A short climb takes you to the highest point of the route, 380 metres ASL. From here follow the superb gravel road downhill for an arm-aching 3 km to reach the B6001.

Turn right and follow the road to **Hassop**, ignoring a minor road that joins from the left just as you enter the village. Follow the road through the village, past the **Eyre Arms** and round the left-hand bend by **Hassop Hall**. 50 metres past the bend and on the left is **Home Farm**. Just past the last of the farm buildings leave the road by a track on the left. The track is identified by an *Unsuitable For Motors* sign and, a few metres up the track, two large gates, side by side. Go through the left-hand gate and straight on to enter a walled section of track. Follow this rutted track, which is very muddy in wet conditions, to a stream. Choose the direct route or 'wimp out' by crossing the small stone bridge on the right.

Ascend the excellent gravel track that climbs straight on and up through **Birchill Bank Woods**, then pleasantly down over fields to meet the **A619**. Turn right and climb to the summit. Turn right again, 14.9 km from the start, along the A6020, signposted *Ashford, Buxton*. Follow the road, going straight on over the roundabout.

400 metres after the roundabout and directly opposite **Toll Bar House**, go through a gate on the left. Cross the field and straight over the Monsal Trail to climb the bridleway. Follow this partly walled track straight on up and over the hill. It enters a wider, grassy section and then joins a gravel track that descends towards **Bakewell**. Pass through a brickyard to a T-junction opposite a small bridge.

Turn left and ride to the **A619**. Turn right and after a couple of hundred metres, turn left into Castle Mount Crescent. Follow the Crescent round to the left to its end at a T-junction. Turn right and ride steeply up to a second T-junction. Turn left into Burre Close and ride down to yet another T-junction. The carpark at Bakewell Station is to your left.

Ascending to Bakewell. (opp.)

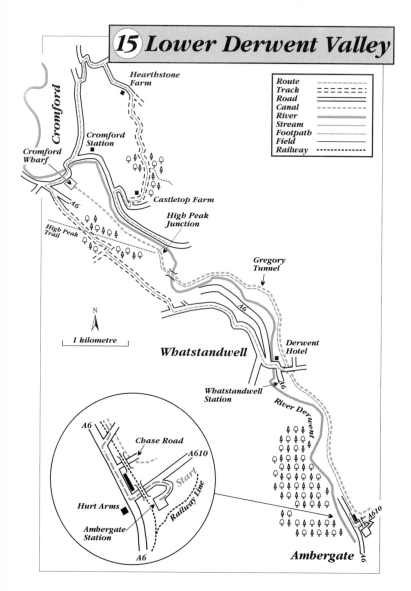

15 Lower Derwent Valley

Route
Track
Road
Canal
River
Stream
Footpath
Field
Railway

Cromford

Hearthstone Farm

Cromford Station

Cromford Wharf

A6

Castletop Farm

High Peak Trail

High Peak Junction

Gregory Tunnel

A6

N

1 kilometre

Whatstandwell

Derwent Hotel

A6

Whatstandwell Station

River Derwent

A6

Chase Road

A610

Start

Hurt Arms

Ambergate Station

Railway Line

A6

A610

Ambergate

A6

15. Lower Derwent Valley

Distance	23 km, 14 miles, 78% off-road.
Time	2 hours.
Map	OS Outdoor Leisure 24 *White Peak*.
Facilities	Shops, cafés and pubs in Ambergate, Cromford and at High Peak Junction.
Rail Access	Ambergate Station. Check the timetable as the trains do not run every day.

Summary

This ride explores the lower Derwent Valley via a canal towpath, enjoyable bridleways with two good descents, and a road section that includes a very steep climb. The valley is very picturesque, especially in spring or autumn. On fine days, particularly in summer, the Cromford Canal towpath is very popular with visitors. For this reason – and because the southern part of Cromford Canal is a nature reserve – a maximum group size of four is recommended for this ride.

The Route

Start in **Ambergate Station** carpark, OS grid ref. 349516. From the carpark ride round the hairpin bend and down to the A610. Turn left to pass under the railway bridge. At the T-junction turn right and ride along the A6 for 500 metres to reach a small tarmac lane on the right just before the de-restricted speed limit signs.

Ride up the lane, crossing over a railway bridge. Just after the bridge go through a gate on the left to join the **Cromford Canal** towpath. *This is a concessionary cycle-way through a nature reserve. Please ride quietly and considerately and give way to pedestrians on the narrow path.*

Follow the towpath northwards for 2.5 km to the stone bridge at **Whatstandwell**. Leave the towpath here by going left on the road and riding down a few metres to the A6 by the **Derwent Hotel**. Cross the bridge, follow the A6 round to the right for a few metres to a junction where two minor roads join the A6 from the left. Turn left up the right-hand road, the **B5035**, signposted *Wirksworth*.

Follow the B5035 for approximately 2 km round bends by **Cupola Park**, and ignoring the tarmac-surfaced, farm access road on the right, signposted *Birchwood Farm*. Carry on along the B5035 for a further 200 metres to reach a bridleway on the right. This track is next to a house named **Wayside Cottage** and is signposted *Public Bridleway to Cromford*.

Follow the bridleway for just over 1 km to a T-junction formed by a sharp left-hand bend in the track and another track joining from the right via a gate. Take the right-hand track, passing through the gate. 100 metres after the gate negotiate a sharp left-hand bend. If you misjudge this bend you will have time to make sure your pilot's licence is up-to-date before you land!

Descend this excellent track (Intake Lane) all the way to Cromford, passing under the **High Peak Trail** *en route*. Near Cromford the track becomes metalled. Follow the tarmac road down to the A6.

Turn left and follow the A6 for 400 metres to traffic lights at the crossroads. Turn right, signposted *Lea, Holloway, Crich*. Ride past **Arkwright's Mill** and **Cromford Wharf** (the northern end of the canal) and follow the road, crossing a bridge over the **River Derwent**.

After the bridge the road swings right past the entrance to **Willersley Castle**. Just after the bend, turn left into Willersley Lane, signposted *Starkholmes, Matlock*. The next section is mainly uphill on tarmac, but the descent is worth the climb. Climb steadily up Willersley Lane conserving as much energy as possible. After 700 metres turn right into White Tor Road, signposted *Unsuitable For Motor Vehicles*. Climb more steeply now to reach a junction with the Starkholmes to Riber road at a hairpin bend. Follow the road right and, after a few metres, right again round another sharp bend. As you tackle the final, very steep climb, forswear tobacco, chocolate or any other vice and consider the fitness of hill climbing cyclists who *race* up this road! The crest of the ridge brings relief and a rest on a convenient boulder.

Follow the road eastwards for 200 metres until a right turn into Hearthstone Lane takes you towards **Hearthstone Farm**. Follow the road past the farm to its end at a cattle grid with a metal gate on its right. Take the sandy, walled track to the right of the gate and climb gently southwards. The track rises over the ridge before beginning an excellent 1 km descent to the valley floor. From this point on the route is either downhill or flat all the way back to Ambergate!

After 500 metres the track forks. Take the right, downhill, fork. Pass through a gate to follow the terraced track as it descends fields and through woods to reach tarmac again by **Castletop Farm**. Turn left and then follow the tarmac steeply down right to meet the Cromford to Lea Bridge minor road. Take care at the bottom; the end arrives very suddenly.

Turn left and follow the road for 1 km before turning right into the **High Peak Junction** carpark. Follow the gravel track left of the gates of **Lea Reclamation Works**. Cross bridges to reach the Information Centre. The helpful wardens will provide information on the Cromford Canal, and on the now defunct High Peak Railway which began its long climb to Buxton from just behind the Visitor Centre. *(The* Bonsall Moor *ride – which starts in the carpark – ascends the long inclines from High Peak Junction.)* Take the canal towpath on the same side as the Information Centre and go south towards the Wharf Sheds. Just after the wharf sheds, the path forks. Take the left fork, signposted *Whatstandwell*.

Follow the towpath for approximately 5 km to reach the gate in **Ambergate** where you joined the towpath near the start of your ride. (If you miss this gate, the rideable section of the canal ends 600 metres further on. Retrace your tracks to the gate.) Leave the canal here by going out onto the lane. Turn right and ride down to the A6. Turn left, ride for 500 metres then turn left again onto the A610. Go right after passing under the bridge and ascend **Ambergate Station** approach road.

Intake Lane; (also opp.)

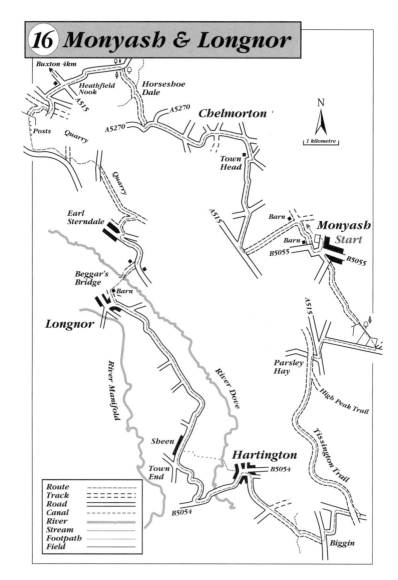

16 Monyash & Longnor

Buxton 4km

Heathfield Nook

Horseshoe Dale

A5270

A5270

Chelmorton

A515

Posts

Quarry

Quarry

Town Head

N

1 kilometre

Earl Sterndale

A515

Barn

Monyash

Start

Barn

B5055

B5055

Beggar's Bridge

Barn

Longnor

River Manifold

River Dove

A515

Parsley Hay

High Peak Trail

Sheen

Tissington Trail

Town End

Hartington

B5054

B5054

Biggin

Route	- - - - -
Track	
Road	
Canal	- - - - -
River	
Stream	
Footpath	
Field	

16. Monyash & Longnor

Distance	50 km, 31 miles, 54% off-road.
Time	6 hours.
Map	OS Outdoor Leisure 24 White Peak.
Facilities	Good pubs en route. Pubs and shop in Longnor (shop opens on Sunday). Cafés, shops, pubs in Hartington. Cycle hire and refreshments at Parsley Hay.
Rail Access	Buxton Station (4 km from Heathfield Nook).

Summary

An excellent ride covering some spectacular and interesting terrain. The challenge lies in its length rather than any sustained technical difficulty or navigational problems. Starting in Monyash the ride circles round the high limestone country of Central Derbyshire and East Staffordshire, dipping into quiet limestone dales and the upper part of the superb Dove Valley. It passes through Longnor and then Hartington – one of the area's 'honey-pot' villages. A section of the Tissington Trail is followed by an old coach road back to Monyash. A compass is highly recommended for this route as one section could give problems in poor visibility.

The Route

Start in **Monyash** at the carpark at OS grid ref. 149666. From the carpark go back to the **B5055** and turn right (west). Follow the main road out of Monyash round a sharp right-hand bend and then, at a sharp left-hand bend with a small stone barn on the corner, go straight on into a gravel track. Follow this track for 900 metres to a track crossroads by a larger stone barn. Turn left and ascend the walled track to meet the **A515** by the **Bull-i'-th'-Thorn** pub.

Turn right and ride for 150 metres to turn right again into a minor road, signposted *Flagg*. Follow this road for nearly 1 km to a junction where two minor roads join from the left. Take the second of these two roads and follow it to a T-junction at **Town Head**. Turn left, signposted *Chelmorton* and ride to a crossroads. Turn left again, also signposted *Chelmorton* and follow this road round sweeping bends to a T-junction with the **A5270**. Turn left, signposted *Brierlow Bar*, and ride for 400 metres to a sharp right-hand bend. In the angle of the bend on the right, a bridleway descends through a farmyard into **Horseshoe Dale**. Follow the dale down for 1 km to where Back Dale joins from the left and craggy Deep Dale curves round rightwards.

Go left for a few metres towards Back Dale then go right through a gate. Ascend the steep and hidden path, at first to the left then to the right as it climbs the precipitous side of the dale. Take care on the exposed upper section or you may experience 'big air' in quantities greater than you ever imagined!

Follow the path straight on across fields to a short section of walled track that curves round to meet a road. Turn left and follow the road to a T-junction. Turn left again and ride along the road to a major crossroads with the A515 at **Heathfield Nook**. Go straight across to a T-junction. Turn left and after 100 metres turn right into the tarmac approach road to an old quarry.

Ascend this road passing through a gap in the embankment of an old railway line. Just after the gap and before the gate go right on a bridleway that climbs up to meet the old railway line. Go left (north-westwards) along the track for 250 metres to where the track starts a right-hand curve and two large limestone boulders partially block the way ahead.

Go left through a gate and ascend the path straight up the steep hillside crossing an old siding and then climbing diagonally rightwards up and round to a gate on the crest of the ridge.

Go left towards a monolithic post standing in the field. From this post further large posts (old railway sleepers) can be seen marking the line of the bridleway across the large field. (This section could give trouble in poor visibility. Follow a bearing of 176 degrees magnetic from the gate and **do not** climb over any walls or fences as there are some very deep quarries hereabouts.)

Descend the field following the line of posts to a gate onto a road. Do not go through the gate, but turn left to ride on tussocks of grass between the fence and the embankment. This section ends at a gate where a rough track leaves the road. Go straight across bearing slightly left to ascend a field to the crest of the hill. Go through a gate into another field overlooking Buxton Quarry. Turn right and, keeping the wall on your right, go down the field to a gate and road.

Go straight across and ascend the wide gravel track along the crest of the ridge. Riding this unique track is a bizarre and thought-provoking experience. One of the most abused parts of Derbyshire lies to your left while the Dove Valley, one of the most serene and picturesque landscapes in the area, lies to your right.

Follow the ridge for 1.8 km to a point approximately 21 km from the start where a broad gravel track cuts back to the right and descends the hillside. Take this fast track to a sharp right-hand bend on the outskirts of Earl Sterndale. Go left and drop down to a lower track. Go left again and follow the track to a road. Turn right and ride down for 100 metres to a T-junction in **Earl Sterndale**. Turn left. (Or turn right if you wish to visit the welcoming pub *The Quiet Woman* which is in the centre of the village on the left.)

Ride down through the narrow defile between Aldery Cliff and High Wheeldon where, on a good day, you might see both rock-climbers and hang-gliders airborne. Ride down to a left-hand bend where a minor road joins from the right. Turn right and ride down the minor road for 100 metres to sharp right-hand bend. Go straight on passing through a gate to enter a broad, grassy, walled track. Follow this down to cross the narrow **Beggar's Bridge** over the **River Dove**.

Ride straight on up the steep bank and across the field towards a barn. Pass to the right of the barn, then go left to a gravel track just past the barn. Go right and ride up the track to meet a minor road on the outskirts of **Longnor**. Go left and follow the road out to a T-junction. (The village centre with shop and pubs is to your right.)

Turn left and ride for 300 metres to a right fork, signposted *Sheen*. Take the right fork and follow this long road along the crest of the ridge between the Dove and Manifold Valleys, through **Sheen** to the first minor road on the left, 5 km from the fork near Longnor, OS grid ref. 109606. *(There is a tempting bridleway that runs eastwards from Sheen down into the Dove Valley. Unfortunately this becomes a footpath on the Derbyshire side of the river and therefore involves 500 metres of pushing.)*

Turn left, signposted *Hartington*, and ride to a T-junction with the **B5054**. Turn left and ride into **Hartington**. Keep to the right through the village centre. As you begin to leave the village, turn right into a minor road which has a telephone box on the corner and is signposted *Youth Hostel 250 yards*.

Climb this road for 100 metres then turn right into another minor road. Ascend steeply, then follow the narrow lane straight on – ignoring tracks to the left and right – to a sharp right-hand bend in the road.

Take the track that goes straight on, signposted *Biggin Dale*, and follow it to a short descent into the dale. Go right and follow the floor of the dale for a couple of hundred metres to a point where a small dale joins from the left. Go left on a narrow path, crossing a low wall, then ascending the dale to a minor road.

Turn left and ride for 200 metres before turning right into another minor road, signposted *Biggin*. Follow this road round a sharp left-hand bend to a T-junction. Turn right into Main Street and ride up the road to pass under a bridge.

Immediately after the bridge go left and ride up a narrow path to the **Tissington Trail**. Go right, north-westwards, and follow the Tissington Trail for approximately 4.7 km to its junction with the **High Peak Trail**. Go left along the High Peak Trail for 300 metres to **Parsley Hay**. Leave the trail at Parsley Hay by going right and riding for a short distance through the carpark to a minor road. Turn left and ride for a few metres to a T-junction with the **A515**. **Take care here – this is a very fast section of road**.

Go left and ride for 50 metres before turning right into a minor road, signposted *Monyash*. Ride for 200 metres to take another turning on the right, signposted *Youlgreave, Lathkill Dale, Arbor Low*. Ride along this road for approximately 1.8 km to a gravelled

Dove Valley.

farm access track on the left, signposted *One Ash Grange* and *Cales Farm*.

Go left over the cattle grid at the start of the gravel track and enter the field. Now ignore the track and ride diagonally leftwards over the field crossing a shallow depression. On ascending the bank on the far side of the depression, two gates – about 15 metres apart and in the corner of the field – become visible. Go through the right-hand of these two gates.

Follow the right-hand (north-easterly) wall down into a very small dale and then up the field to a gate in the corner of the field.

Go through the gate and straight on down the broad, grassy walled track. This track – Derby Lane – becomes tarmac on the outskirts of **Monyash** and then joins a minor road at a bend. Go straight on across the **B5055** to find the carpark on the left. Congratulations – you have just completed the longest ride in this book!

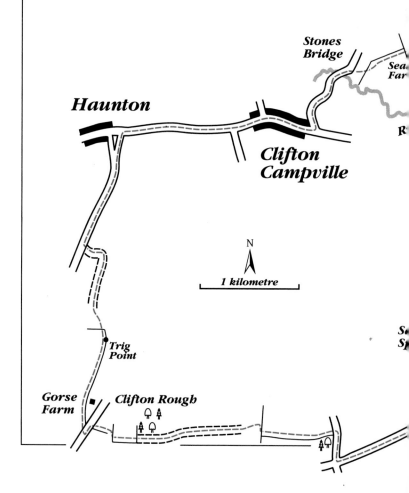

17 Netherseal~ Four Counties

Stones Bridge

Sea Far

Haunton

Clifton Campville

R

N

1 kilometre

S *S*

● **Trig Point**

Gorse Farm

Clifton Rough

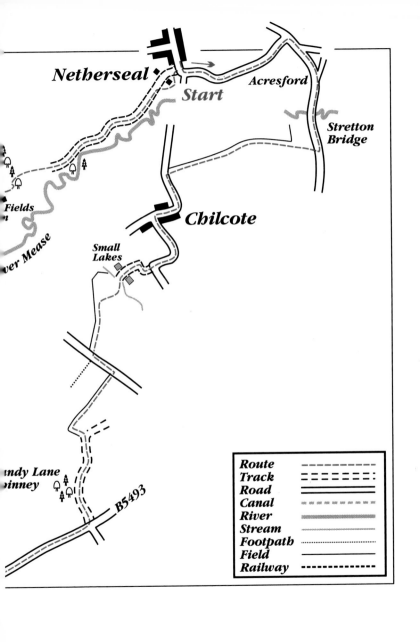

Netherseal

Start

Acresford

Stretton
Bridge

Fields

ver Mease

Chilcote

Small
Lakes

ndy Lane
pinney

B5493

Route	---------
Track	- - - - -
Road	=========
Canal	= = = = =
River	=========
Stream	---------
Footpath	·········
Field	---------
Railway	-·-·-·-·-

17. Netherseal – Four Counties

Distance	25 km, 15.5 miles, 52% off-road.
Time	2 hours.
Maps	OS Pathfinder 893 *Tamworth* & 873 *Ashby-de-la-Zouch*.
Facilities	Shop & pub in Netherseal.
Rail Access	Not practical.

Summary

A ride through rich, rolling farmland and small red-brick villages that starts in the extreme south of Derbyshire then crosses into Leicestershire, Warwickshire and Staffordshire. Although there are no steep hills this route is quite demanding as field riding often is. For this reason it would be best to do this route after a long dry spell or when the ground is frozen. Muddy conditions would be very wearing.

Some of the bridleways cross directly over cropped fields. Often the way will have been made visible by previous users but, if this is not the case, common sense and the edge of fields should be used to avoid crop damage.

The Route

Start in the village of **Netherseal** at OS grid ref. 287128 on sheet 873 *Ashby-de-la-Zouch*. Park in Main Street near the **Holly Bush**.

From the Holly Bush go south for a few metres until the road turns left (east) by a stone cross and becomes Church Street. Follow Church Street to the junction with the A444 by the **Cricketts Inn**. Turn right and ride along the busy **A444**. Descend into a shallow valley and cross the River Mease at **Stretton Bridge**. 300 metres after crossing the river, and at a point approximately 1.9 km from the start, find a solitary wooden signpost – with a picture of a horse shoe – pointing across a field on your right.

Cross straight over the field towards hedges that mark the outside corner of another field by a junction of power lines. This corner is 200 metres from the road. From the corner go left along the hedge in more or less the same direction you have been riding. Go straight on into another field crossing a small bridge made from wooden railway sleepers and marked by a wooden post with bridleway arrows. Ride along the right field boundary to the corner. Cross into a third field and carry straight on, but now keeping the hedge on your left. Follow this to a minor road.

Turn left and follow the road round into the village of **Chilcote**. Turn left by the church into *No Mans Heath Road*. Follow this road round a sharp right-hand bend. Then at the next bend, a sharp left-hand bend, go straight on through a bridlegate next to large double gates onto a gravel farm track. After a few metres the track curves right. In theory the bridleway goes straight on but it would seem better to follow the track rightwards and then after a few more metres turn left along another track that parallels the original bridleway.

Follow this track, crossing a short causeway between two small lakes, then passing between two rough stone posts into a huge field.

The walls and hedges marked on the OS map have been removed. Depending on the state and type of crops, crossing this field may require some ingenuity! The point you are heading for is where the remaining hedge on the right (west) of the field meets the road at the top of the slope. It is on a bearing of 206 degrees from the two rough stone posts. The best course seems to be to follow any track that leads into the centre of the field and then turn right heading for the hedge on the right. Follow this hedge up to the road.

Turn left and ride for 200 metres to a road junction on the left with a small grass triangle. Opposite this junction on your right is a bridlegate. Go through the gate and follow the right hedge to the next corner. Turn left and follow another hedge for a short distance to cross straight over a concrete farm track and into **Sandy Lane** – a broad gravel track.

Ride along Sandy Lane to a crossroads with the **B5493**. Turn right. Ride for 1.7 km to another crossroads. Turn right, signposted *Thorpe Constantine* and *Clifton Campville*.

Ride for 300 metres until, just after a gentle right-hand bend, a bridlegate is found on the left. Go through the gate and follow the left-hand field boundary to another gate in the corner. Pass through this gate.

Move right a few metres and follow the right side of a hedge in the centre of the field. Follow this hedge to its end and go through a bridlegate in the hedge to emerge on a track.

Turn right and ride for only 15 metres to a wooden signpost that points the way straight across the field to your left. Cross the field to meet an obvious gravel track that continues in the same direction towards Clifton Rough – a small wood. Follow the track under power lines and into the edge of **Clifton Rough**. Go straight on following the now more overgrown track through the wood to a field.

Follow the left-hand hedge to the corner. Pass through another bridlegate onto a road. Go diagonally leftwards across the road to find a bridlegate next to a large double gate.

Go into the field and follow the right field boundary. Keep going straight on for nearly a kilometre to a **trig. point**.

200 metres after the trig. point, and in the corner of the field, pass through a gap in the hedge and go straight on over the field towards a prominent tree on the far side.

Pass to the left of the tree and then follow the left side of the hedge directly behind it. Go into the next field, carrying on in the same direction. On the far side of this field, turn left into a wide, muddy track between hedges. Follow this track to a small tarmac lane.

Turn right and ride into **Haunton**. When the road forks, go right and then at the T-junction go right again. Ride for approximately 1.8 km to **Clifton Campville**. Ride straight through the village, ignoring the first minor road on the left. On the far side of the village turn left into Netherseal Lane, signposted *Netherseal*. This junction is 18.5 km from the start of the ride. Ride for 700 metres to a bridge over the **River Mease**.

On the right a few metres after the bridge, a wooden bridleway signpost points the way across the field. Go diagonally left across the field (heading just to the right of the farm buildings on the horizon) towards a gap in the far hedge. Cross a small bridge over the large ditch and pass into another field.

The bridleway goes directly across the field but it is better to go left and follow the edge of the field round to the top (north-east) corner to the left of the farm buildings.

Ascend a small bank to cross a concrete farm track about 150 metres north of the **Seal Fields Farm**. Go straight on, crossing the field on a track. Follow this track to the corner of the field and then go left, skirting a narrow band of trees. 70 metres past the corner a gap appears in the trees on your right. Go through the gap and straight on down the gently sloping field on the other side. Cross into the next field by a weathered wooden gatepost with a bridleway arrow.

Go straight on again, heading towards a small wood. Skirt the wood on its left side, then ride beside the river on a well-used path. Follow this path along the edge of successive fields in generally the same direction you have been travelling.

This path eventually becomes a wide, grassy bridleway between hedges. Follow this to a point about 150 metres before **Hall Farm** – a red-brick farm that appears to block the way ahead. On the right is a gate into a paddock. Go through the gate and cross three small fields towards the farm. After the third field a very short walled section leads to a track. Turn right and ride a few metres to the stone cross at the junction of Main Street and Church Street in **Netherseal**. Turn left and ride for a few metres to the Holly Bush.

River Mease.

Near Seal Fields Farm. (opp.)

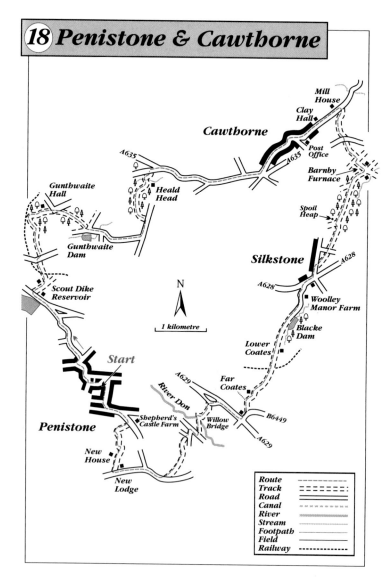

18 Penistone & Cawthorne

Mill House

Clay Hall

Cawthorne

A635

Post Office

A635

Barnby Furnace

Gunthwaite Hall

Heald Head

Spoil Heap

Silkstone

A628

Gunthwaite Dam

A628

Scout Dike Reservoir

Woolley Manor Farm

Blacke Dam

Lower Coates

N

1 kilometre

Start

A629

Far Coates

River Don

Willow Bridge

B6449

Penistone

Shepherd's Castle Farm

A629

New House

New Lodge

Route	------
Track	========
Road	———
Canal	
River	
Stream	
Footpath	·········
Field	
Railway	--------

18. Penistone & Cawthorne

Distance	28 km, 17 miles, 57% off-road.
Time	3 hours.
Map	OS Outdoor Leisure 1 *Dark Peak*. (Not shown on older editions).
Facilities	Pubs *en route*.
Rail Access	Penistone Station.

Summary

A straightforward route through attractive Yorkshire farmland on the north-western edge of the Peak District. In dry conditions the rolling terrain and easy surfaces are kind to the mountain biker. However, like many 'lowland' routes, in wet conditions some of the tracks become sticky so the ride requires significantly more time and energy. The bridleways are well-signposted and there are no navigational problems.

The Route

Start in **Penistone** at the carpark in Shrewsbury Road next to the Metro Cinema, OS grid ref. 248032. From the carpark go out onto the road, turn left and ride up the hill towards the church. At the T-junction turn right and follow the road down and round to traffic lights. Turn right on the A628 then take the first turning left, the B6462, Huddersfield Road. At a T-junction turn left onto the **A629** Halifax Road.

Ride for 300 metres, then take the signposted bridleway on the right just past **Scout Dike Outdoor Centre**. Ride for 300 metres along this track. Just past **Carr Lodge Farm** turn left along a bridleway. Pass to the right of the brick building and follow a narrower path over the railway to a minor road.

Turn right and after only 50 metres turn left on a bridleway. Follow this path straight on through a gate and on to a wider track. Keep going straight on across fields to a short descent which ends at the small brook at **Clough Bridge**. Cross the bridge and follow the track up through the farmyard of **Gunthwaite Hall** to a minor road and path junction. Take the bridleway to the right, named on a signpost as *Gunthwaite Lane*. This appealing track must be one of the longest sections of stone-paved bridleway in the region, although recently it has been edged with gravel for the benefit of equestrians.

Gunthwaite Lane ends at a triple road junction. Go straight on, passing to the left of a small reservoir. Ignore the first turning on the right and ride on to a T-junction. Turn left and ride for 300 metres to a wide gravel track on the left. Follow this highly enjoyable walled track down and round to the right over increasingly large logs placed across the track for the benefit of equestrians and ambitious mountain bikers. Eventually, after passing **Heald Head**, the track crosses two excellent fords and ends at a minor road.

Turn right and, after a few metres, right again onto the A635. Ride for 2.3 km to the second road on the left. This junction is marked by a millstone – inscribed *Cawthorne* – set in the verge on the left. Follow this road to and through **Cawthorne**. Keep to the left at Cawthorne Post Office and ride along Darton Road.

Leaving the village, pass **Clay Hall** and ride on to **Mill House**. 150 metres past Mill House (approximately 12.7 km from the start) and on the right, a bridleway climbs a sunken path. Follow this to a road. Go straight across into a pleasant walled track and ride to a track crossroads. Swing right and then left, going straight on through the junction. Descend to **Furnace Bridge**. Turn right opposite the house and beside the black corrugated-iron barn.

Follow this long, fast track keeping to the left at the first fork and then turning left into a slightly narrower track opposite some low black spoil heaps. Go straight across a minor road on the outskirts of **Silkstone** passing alongside the approach road to a new estate. Keep going straight on behind the **Ring Of Bells** pub to emerge at a road near a major T-junction.

Turn left and ride to the T-junction. Turn right on the **A628**, signposted *Penistone*. Follow the main road for 300 metres before veering left into Blackergreen Lane. This lane becomes a bridleway by **Blacke Dam**. Keep going straight on, pausing only to admire the mystic sculpture by the gate near **Lower Coates**.

A long, steady climb ends at **Far Coates**. Ignore a track that merges from the left. Go right past the farm then follow the drive round to the left and out to a minor road. Turn right and ride down to a crossroads by the **Travellers Inn**. Turn right and ride up for 500 metres to the top of the hill. Turn left, signposted *Willow Lane Farm*, and after 100 metres turn left again, passing to the left of the farm buildings on a signposted bridleway.

This fast, narrow descent has a sharp bend at the bottom. Ride down to, and across, **Willow Bridge** – a packhorse bridge over the **River Don**. Follow the track left and up to a road. Turn right and ride for only 100 metres before turning left into a tarmac side road. A few metres up this road and on the right is a side road called Psalters Drive. The bridleway leaves the road at this junction. Go up the grassy track, crossing a bridge over an old railway line and following the track up through fields. The surface eventually becomes tarmac near **Sycamore Farm**. Go straight on through the centre gate to follow the walled gravel track. Keep going straight on past **Root House Farm** to meet a minor road at **Tenyard Farm**.

Turn right. Ignore the first road that joins from the left, but take the next, Oxspring Road, on the left. Ride for 600 metres to a bridleway on the right just past **New Lodge**. Follow this wide, fast track downhill. Where it swings left into **New House** go straight on, then go round left and right-hand bends to **New House Farm**. Stay on the track to meet tarmac at **Shepherd's Castle Farm**. Turn left and at the T-junction turn left again. Ride beside a foundry and take the next turning on the right, Ward Street.

Take the next road right (unnamed) then turn right again into another unnamed road that passes Penistone Church Football Club. Ride down to a T-junction. Turn left and follow the road for 100 metres round to the left and back to the carpark.

Traffic jam near Gunthwaite Hall.

Ford near Heald Head. (opp.)

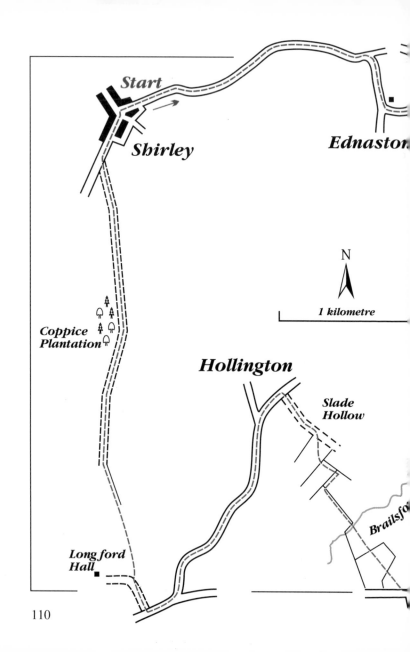

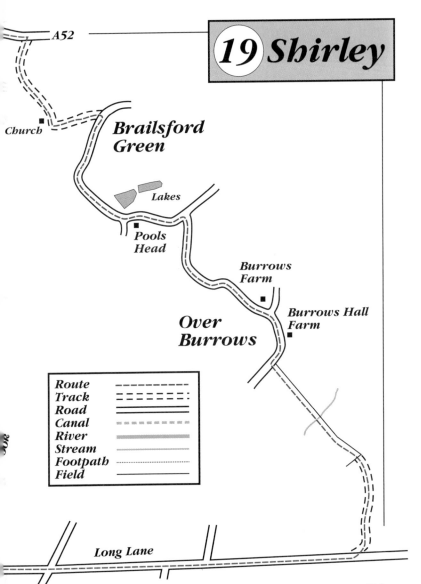

A52

Church

Brailsford Green

Lakes

Pools Head

Burrows Farm

Burrows Hall Farm

Over Burrows

Route	----
Track	====
Road	——
Canal	- - -
River	▓▓▓
Stream	——
Footpath	····
Field	——

Long Lane

19. Shirley

Distance	18 km, 11 miles, 44% off-road.
Time	2 hours.
Map	OS Pathfinder Nos. 811 *Belper* and 832 *Derby &* *Etwall*. (See note in Summary.)
Facilities	Good pubs *en route*.
Rail Access	Not practical.

Summary

Mainly easy field and track riding through farmland to the west of Derby. There are hawthorn hedges so make sure you have spare inner tubes and a good repair kit. There is one section where the route is not obvious on the ground, so carrying the 1:25 000 maps should be regarded as essential. Although there are few hills on this ride, it does cover some interesting ground and this, plus the excellent pubs make it an enjoyable experience on a warm summer evening.

The Route

Start in the centre of **Shirley** at OS grid ref. 219416 (OS Sheet 811 *Belper*). There is limited space; please park carefully to avoid blocking access to drives, etc.

Find Derby Lane, the main road eastwards from Shirley to Ednaston. Follow Derby Lane eastwards for nearly 2 km to turn right into a minor road, signposted *Ednaston*. This turning is a few metres before the junction with the A52.

Ride into **Ednaston** to turn left just past the **Yew Tree Inn**, signposted *Brailsford*. Follow this to a crossroads with the **A52**. Turn right, signposted *Derby & Brailsford*, and – crossing **Brailsford Brook** *en route* – ride for 100 metres to turn right into a tarmac farm track. Where the track veers left go straight on through the gate and follow the rough track to **Brailsford Church**.

From the church follow the tarmac drive leftwards to a road. Turn right and ride past a small lake on the left to a junction on a right-hand bend near **Pools Head**. Turn left and ride along this narrow lane to take the first minor road on the right. Follow this lane through a gate and round a left-hand bend. At a sharp right-hand bend go straight on through another gate and ride through **Over Burrows** to a T-junction.

Turn right and ride for approximately 400 metres passing **Burrows Hall Farm** to the start of a signposted bridleway that leaves the road via a gate into a field on the left. Follow the left boundary of this field and the next one straight down to a bridge over a brook.

Cross the bridge into the next field. The bridleway goes straight on up the field – passing a solitary oak tree – to a gate on the right-hand side of a short section of hedge and ditch which is all that remains of the original field boundary. (This field may be planted. Use your discretion to minimise crop damage.) Pass through the gate and follow the hedged path to a wider grassy track which leads to a tarmac drive by **Twenty Acres**.

Go straight on and follow the drive out to **Long Lane** (a Roman Road). Turn right (start counting the minor roads on the left) and follow Long Lane for approximately 2.7 km passing the **Three Horse Shoes** on the way.

At the junction with the fourth minor road on the left after joining Long Lane (and at a point 450 metres past the crossroads at **Stoop Farm**) go right into a field. The bridleway is not well-marked. Use your map and some ingenuity to find the route. The bridleway goes diagonally leftwards to cross into the next field over a fence and ditch. (A gate is scheduled to be installed here.) Cross the next field towards a gate in the far corner.

Pass through the gate and follow the edge of this field leftwards and then round to the right to a substantial bridge across **Brailsford Brook**. Cross the bridge and go straight up the field – keeping the hedge on your right – to a gate in the top right-hand corner. Go through the gate into the field on the right and follow the hedge on the left to another gate. Go through this gate and ascend the field

Roman Lakes Café.

into yet another field. Go diagonally right down to a gate that gives access to a track at **Slade Hollow**.

Turn left and follow the track to a road in **Hollington**. Turn left and then go left again where a more major road joins from the right. Follow the road through **Hollington Grove** to meet **Long Lane** again. Turn right and ride for approximately 200 metres to turn right into the tarmac drive of **Longford Hall**, signposted *Parish Church*.

Follow the drive for 150 metres to a left-hand bend just before a bridge. Leave the drive here by passing though a gate on the right. Beyond the gate go diagonally leftwards across the field, ascending gently to a solitary gate on the far side.

Go through (or round!) this gate and ride along a raised bank keeping the hedge on your right. Carry straight on through a gate and enter a hedged track which is followed for nearly 2 km to tarmac. Go straight on to meet a minor road. Turn right and ride up into the centre of **Shirley** where you started your ride.

Coppice Plantation near Shirley.

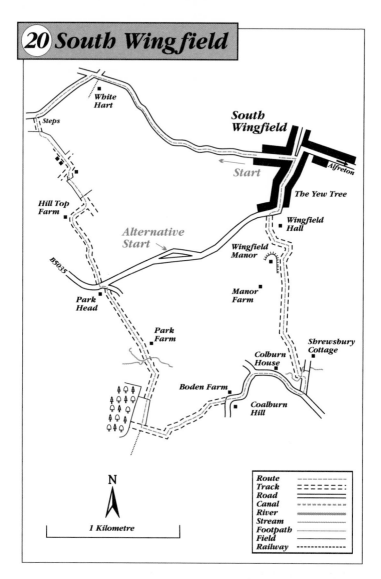

20. South Wingfield

Distance	8 km, 5 miles, 63% off-road.
Time	1 hour.
Map	OS Pathfinder 794 *Crich and Bullbridge*.
Facilities	Pubs and shops in South Wingfield.
Rail Access	Ambergate Station (5.5 km from Shrewsbury Cottage)

Summary

A short and easy ride over Edge Moor and through Wingfield Park that makes for a pleasant evening or short day. Straightforward navigation and no real technical difficulty make this an ideal introduction for those new to off-road cycling. The route features one moderate, narrow climb, a good and reasonably long descent and good views of the Amber Valley. The ride passes Wingfield Manor House which is worth a visit.

The Route

Start in Inns Lane, OS grid ref. 375555, about 100 metres west of the junction with the B5035 in the village of South Wingfield.

Follow Inns Lane westwards for 1.6 km to the staggered crossroads by the **White Hart** pub. Turn left into Wild Lane, signposted *Crich*. Follow Wild Lane for approximately 600 metres. Just after a right-hand bend where the road steepens slightly, a bridleway leaves the road on the left. Climb up the three wooden-edged steps and up the narrow path to reach a bridlegate at the corner of a field. Follow the left, east, boundary of the field with good views across the Amber Valley. Pass between the fences and to the left of the new barn.

Go straight on past a gap between two barns, then follow the track as it swings right then left through the farmyard to reach a wooden gate with a squeeze on its left. Go through the gate to follow the

117

obvious semi-tarmac track that parallels the right boundary of the field. At the far side of the field, enter a walled continuation of the track. Follow this track curving right then left past **Hilltop Farm**. As you round the left-hand bend the ruins of the historical Wingfield Manor are visible to the east. Follow the track to the B5035 at **Park Head**.

Cross the B5035 diagonally leftwards into Park Lane, signposted *Wingfield Park, Pentrich*. A few metres along Park Lane on the right, a bridleway leaves the road via a short concrete drive to the left of an outbuilding. A few metres down the drive on the left, a gate with a gritstone squeeze on its left gives access to the bridleway. Cross the field heading for the entrance to a walled track. Follow this to **Park Farm**.

Carry straight on over the concrete apron and down to a shallow ford. This section can be very 'muddy' especially after milking time. Climb up a few metres ignoring a gate on your left and another on your right before reaching two gates side by side and facing you. The left-hand of these two gates has a stile on its left. Pass through this gate, or over the stile if you are feeling fit or have an alloy framed bike. Follow the right wall of the field round into a walled track which climbs gently. Ignore any opening into fields on the left and follow the right wall to reach another pair of gates.

Pass through the right-hand gate and continue up the walled track to enter a field near a fine oak tree. The track across the field is less well-defined. Stick to the left-hand wall until reaching a gate which gives access to another walled track. Turn left down the track, ignoring the footpath which carries straight on, and the footpath to the right. Follow this track down to a wooden gate at a sharp left-hand bend. After the gate turn left and stay with the excellent track downhill all the way to meet a minor road at **Boden Farm**.

Follow the tarmac left for 150 metres to reach a T-junction. Turn right, signposted *Pentrich*. Pass **Colburn House** on your left. The next turning on the left, 250 metres from the T-junction, is a tarmac drive with stone posts and a wooden gate. Go through the gate to

Near Park Farm.

follow the drive until just before the entrance to **Shrewsbury Cottage,** where a walled track on the left leaves the tarmac. Take the track and almost immediately cross a small ford. Follow the track as it curves right and climbs steadily. Pass through a gate and continue along the track below **Wingfield Manor House**, (where the imprisoned Mary Queen of Scots pined and plotted more than 400 years ago), to reach double wooden gates with a stile on their right.

Escape through the gates and flee down the sunken track to your right. Follow this track through a gate and left, to pass an old walled garden by **Wingfield Hall**. Climb to meet the B5035 in **South Wingfield**. Turn right and follow the tarmac up into the centre of the village. Turn left into Inns Lane and so back to your starting point.

21 Three Shires Head & Macclesfield Forest

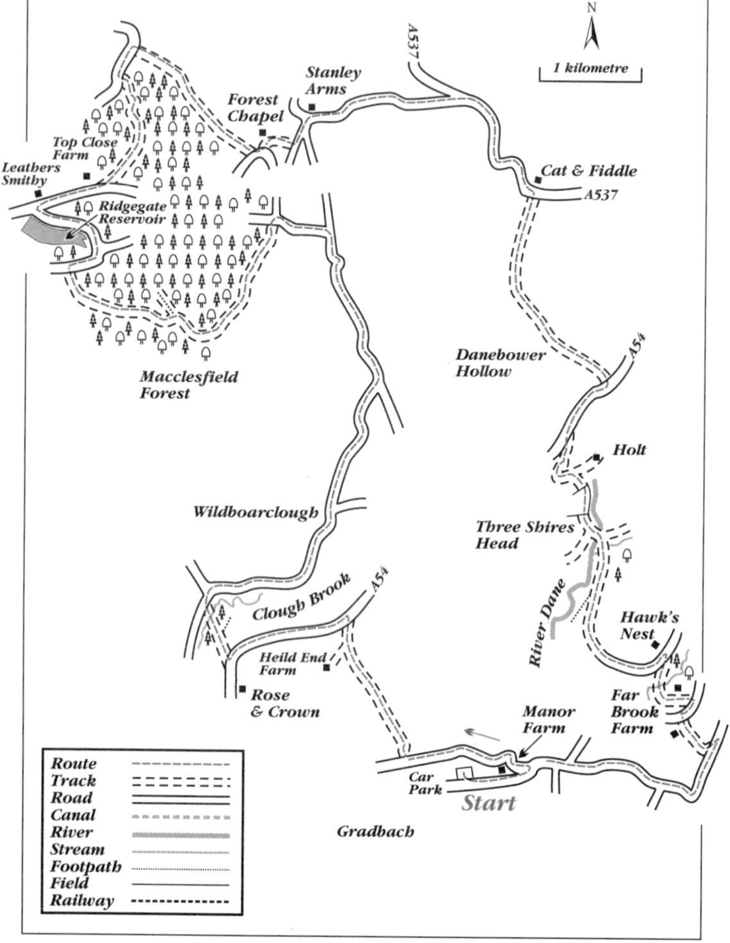

N

1 kilometre

A537

Stanley
Arms

Forest
Chapel

Top Close
Farm

Leathers
Smithy

Ridgegate
Reservoir

Cat & Fiddle
A537

Macclesfield
Forest

Danebower
Hollow

A54

Holt

Wildboarclough

Three Shires
Head

Clough Brook

A54

River Dane

Hawk's
Nest

Heild End
Farm

Rose
& Crown

Manor
Farm

Far
Brook
Farm

Car
Park

Start

Gradbach

Route	- - - - - - -
Track	= = = = = = =
Road	————
Canal	
River	
Stream	
Footpath	....
Field	
Railway	- - - - - - - - -

120

21. Three Shires Head & Macclesfield Forest

Distance	35 km, 22 miles, 54% off-road.
Time	5 hours.
Map	OS Outdoor Leisure 24 *White Peak*.
Facilities	Pubs *en route*. Teas at Far Brook Farm.
Rail Access	Not practical.

Summary

A combination of length, technical ascents and descents, and fast open tracks all contribute to a demanding and memorable ride through terrain as varied and interesting as the ride itself. Starting low down in Gradbach, the route ascends to Macclesfield Forest and drops down towards Langley before climbing over to Forest Chapel. The climb up to the Cat and Fiddle is followed by an exposed section of open moorland which ends with the descent into Danebower Hollow. The Dane Valley is followed to Three Shires Head, where swimming costumes and towels will be useful on hot days. An ascent from here leads to a tricky descent and a climb to Far Brook. One off-road section remains before the last descent to Gradbach. A very good ride.

The Route

Start at the carpark in **Gradbach**, OS grid ref. 999663. From the carpark return eastwards along the lane towards the Flash to Allgreave minor road. At the T-junction near **Manor Farm** turn left, west, and ride towards Allgreave. Ascend steadily. Just after the crest of the first hill, approximately 1.7 km from the start of the ride, turn right into a walled track that has a *No cars, no motorcycles* sign. Follow this track through gates to open fields. Carry on along the track. It descends to meet a tarmac farm track by **Heild End Farm**. Go right and down to the A54. Turn left and follow the A54 downhill for 1.4 km to the start of a track on the right approximately 4.5 km from the start of the ride. This track leaves the road approx. 200 metres *before* the **Rose and Crown**, a pub situated at the next junction.

Follow the track to where it forks, just before a cattle grid. Go left and down a rougher track that descends to the River Dane. Follow the track to a ford. If the river is high a snorkel may be useful! If the ford is too deep to cross, you will need to **push and carry** your bike to and over the footbridge a few metres to the north. On the far side of the river follow the track to the right and out to the road.

Turn right and ascend on tarmac to a junction. Go right, signposted *Wildboarclough*. Ride for approximately 4.5 km through **Wildboarclough**, ignoring two minor roads on the right, to take the first minor road on the left, signposted *Forest Chapel*.

Climb to the crest of the ridge, a short and sharp ascent which ends at a junction where a memorial to Walter Smith on a gritstone slab on the right bears an appropriate quote from Burns.

From this junction take the concessionary bridleway left, south-south-west, signposted *Shutlingsloe* into **Macclesfield Forest**. The track ascends in a series of short climbs to a ridge. After the crest follow the track down to a point approx. 13.6 km from the start of the ride where the bridleway leaves the main track and ascends steeply leftwards, signposted *Trenterbank via Nessit Hill*. Ascend this demoralisingly steep but mercifully short climb and continue on the forest track which soon leads to a satisfyingly long and fast descent.

The descent ends at a road. Turn right and follow the road for 400 metres to a T-junction. Turn left, signposted *Langley and Macclesfield* and ride beside **Ridgegate Reservoir** to a right turning by **Leathers Smithy**. Turn right and ascend this road to a find a concessionary bridleway on the left just after the entrance to **Top Close Farm** and approximately 17.2 km from the start of the ride.

Follow the wide track up into the forest ignoring a gated track on the right and then another on the left. Go straight up past a derelict barn following signposts for *Walker Barn*

Ascend to a minor road. Turn right and ride up to the brow of the hill and turn right again into a gravel track marked by a faded dead-end sign. Follow this excellent track as it skirts the eastern edge of Macclesfield Forest with good views eastwards towards Shining Tor and the Cat & Fiddle which can be seen on the horizon. This rough track ends at a road junction by **Forest Chapel**.

Turn immediately left to ride towards the chapel. Just past the chapel on the right, take the track that leaves the road on the right just before the farmyard. Follow this track down a tricky little descent to a minor road.

Turn left and ride to a T-junction. Turn left again and ride to another T-junction where a right turn, signposted *Buxton*, takes you past the **Stanley Arms**. Ride steadily uphill on tarmac for 1.8 km to a T-junction with the A537. Turn right, signposted *Buxton*, and ride for another 800 metres to the **Cat & Fiddle**, reputed to be the highest pub in the area, which – if you think about it – has to be good news.

Directly opposite the Cat & Fiddle a bridleway leaves the road and crosses the open moor in a roughly southerly direction. Follow this long track through **Danebower Hollow** to meet the **A54** road. Turn right and ride for 600 metres to turn left down a tarmac farm access road which leads to **Holt**.

At a sharp left-hand bend in the farm access track which is just before the farm, leave the tarmac for a short, signposted section of walled bridleway on the right. This soon enters a field. Follow the grassy sunken track down to the left to a gate. Go through the gate and follow the left field boundary round and down to another gate. Go through the gate and cross a small gorge. Continue along the narrow path beside the **River Dane** to the bridge at **Three Shires Head**. There is a waterfall here and, below the bridge, a very tempting pool – a good, but popular, place for lunch and a swim.

Cross the bridge and turn right, crossing another small bridge. Follow the true left bank southwards on a wide path above the River Dane. Pass through a gate. Just after the gate the track forks. Take the left fork that ascends gently round the hillside. This track becomes tarmac.

Follow the tarmac to **Hawks Nest** where it descends slightly, and on the left on the hillside above the lane is a small house with a barn on either side.

On the right-hand side of the road, opposite the small house, a very rough path cuts back southwards alongside the steep overgrown gully. Go down this difficult path into the gully to cross a stream via a small bridge (or a ford) where a footpath crosses your path. Go straight on climbing gently to a gate and stile.

Go through the gate and follow the path up to **Far Brook Farm** where Mrs. Gillian Beard will supply tea and cakes to weary cyclists on Saturday and Sunday – and weekdays by appointment!

Leave Far Brook Farm by ascending the steep concrete drive to the road. Turn right and ride for 50 metres to a signposted grassy bridleway on the left with an unusual mailbox at the bottom. Ascend this bridleway for a few metres to another concrete farm track. Ascend the track to the farm. Ignore the wide track that curves left to the barn, but go straight on, ascending into a field through a gate. Follow the right field boundary to another gate. Pass through the gate and follow the left field boundary of the next field to a track and gate in the wall. Go left through the gate and follow the track to and through a farmyard. Continue to a road.

Turn right and ride downhill for 2 km to turn left into the third minor road on the left, signposted *Gradbach*. Ride for 250 metres back to the carpark where you began your ride.

pproaching Three Shires Head.

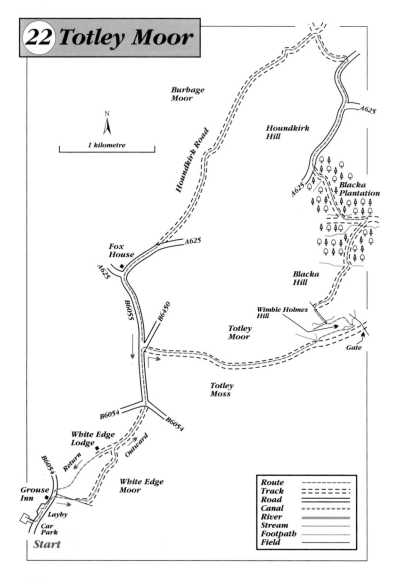

22 Totley Moor

Burbage Moor

N

1 kilometre

Houndkirk Road

Houndkirk Hill

A625

Blacka Plantation

A625

Fox House

A625

B6055

B6450

Blacka Hill

Wimble Holmes Hill

Totley Moor

Gate

Totley Moss

B6054

B6054

White Edge Lodge

Outward

Return

B6054

Grouse Inn

Layby

White Edge Moor

Car Park

Start

Route	-------
Track	=======
Road	
Canal	
River	
Stream	
Footpath	
Field	

22. Totley Moor

Distance	16 km, 10 miles, 85% off-road.
Time	2 hours.
Map	OS Outdoor Leisure 24 *White Peak* & 1 *Dark Peak* (not shown on older editions of *Dark Peak*).
Facilities	Pubs *en route*.
Rail Access	Totley Station (4 km from Blacka Plantation).

Summary

The area of the Peak District National Park immediately west of Sheffield contains an unusual variety of scenery within a compact area. This ride explores this region of fields, woods and open moorland on tracks and paths which vary as much as the landscape itself. Although relatively short, it is quite demanding. The ascent through Blacka Plantation is challenging and parts of the ride are high and exposed; but they are balanced by some fine descents and very unusual paths. A very enjoyable ride.

The Route

Start at the lay-by at OS grid ref. 258779 (*White Peak* map) which is about 50 metres south-west of the Grouse Inn on the B6054. If this lay-by is full there is a carpark a few hundred metres down the B6054.

From the lay-by ride up the road past the **Grouse Inn**. 50 metres after the Grouse go through a gate on the right of the road and follow a vague path diagonally up the field to a gate in the corner.

Go through the gate and ascend a path through birch woodland to a path T-junction. Turn left on a narrow grassy path that ascends across the face of **White Edge**. Follow this path along the edge to reach a gate and stile. Go through the gate and continue traversing along White Edge on a gently ascending path to an open field by

127

White Edge Lodge. Join a broader gravel track then go right and follow it to a road junction where the **B6054** meets the **B6055**.

Go straight across onto the B6055. After 500 metres turn right onto the B6450, signposted *Sheffield*, and then almost immediately go right through a gate and onto a track across open moorland. Cross **Totley Moss** on this track passing an air shaft for Totley Tunnel on the way. Follow the main track straight on where a footpath joins from the left. At a point approximately 4.4 km from the start of the ride, three paths join from the left. The first path cuts back left. The second is at right angles to the track and the third diverges from the track diagonally leftwards towards Sheffield which can now be seen in the distance. Take this third track and follow it round a small bank in roughly the same direction as the main track.

The path rejoins the main track after a few hundred meters. **Just before** rejoining the main track, go left and drop down for 5 metres into the top of a small gully. Then find the narrow path going left that crosses a small stream in the bed of the gully. Cross the stream and continue on the very narrow path as it contours round the end of **Wimble Holme Hill**. (This path can be seen from the junction.)

Follow this exciting path across the steep face of Wimble Holme Hill to its end where it descends to a gate. Go through the gate, cross a small stream and ride up the field next to the wall towards a small stand of trees.

On reaching the trees, go right through a gate onto a broad, lumpy track through bracken and birch scrub. Go straight on down the track which improves to a narrower and smoother section before ending at a path junction by a gap in a dry-stone wall. Go through the gap and follow the well-defined gravel path down into the birch woodland of **Blacka Plantation**.

Follow this brilliant descent through the woods to a stream at the bottom. Ford the stream and turn immediately left between gritstone posts and follow the path for 100 metres to another path junction, approximately 6.6 km from the start.

Go right over a small bridge and follow the wooded path, signposted *Devil's Elbow Gate*. (This path is littered with tree roots and parts of it become a stream bed in very wet conditions; however it has all been ridden when in a reasonably dry state.) Climb this difficult and strenuous path through attractive woodland, ascending to a path junction. Go straight on, signposted *Devil's Elbow Gate*.

Emerge from the wood onto the **A625**. Turn right and ride for 700 metres to turn left into Sheephill Road. Ride for 250 metres to the start of a signposted byway that climbs the hillside on the left.

Ride up this sandy path across bracken moorland to a major path and track junction. Turn left, south-west, onto Houndkirk Road and follow it for nearly 3 km to meet the A625 again.

Turn right and ride down the hill to the bend by the **Fox House**, a pub. Turn left here onto the B6055 and follow it to rejoin your outward route at the B6450 junction. Retrace your outward route to the B6055/B6054 junction.

Go straight on passing through the gate and onto the approach track for **White Edge Lodge**. This time follow the track rightwards towards the Lodge. Pass it on the left and find a wide grassy track that descends across a tussocky field to the **B6054**. Turn left and ride down to the very pleasant **Grouse Inn**. (*Watch out for the deep gravel in the carpark – the cause of some embarrassment to the author!*)

The lay-by (or carpark) where you began the ride is a few metres further on.

Houndkirk Road.

Passing White Edge Lodge. (opp.)

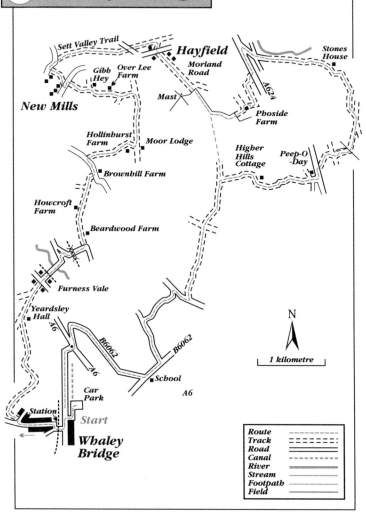

Sett Valley Trail

Hayfield

Stones House

Gibb Hey

Over Lee Farm

Morland Road

A624

New Mills

Mast

Phoside Farm

Hollinhurst Farm

Moor Lodge

Higher Hills Cottage

Peep-O -Day

Brownhill Farm

Howcroft Farm

Beardwood Farm

Furness Vale

Yeardsley Hall

A6

B6062

B6062

N

1 kilometre

School

A6

Car Park

Station

Start

Whaley Bridge

Route	---- ---- ----
Track	========
Road	———
Canal	⎯ ⎯ ⎯
River	▬▬▬▬
Stream	————
Footpath	··········
Field	

23. Whaley Bridge

Distance	26 km, 16 miles, 69% off-road.
Time	4 hours.
Map	OS Outdoor Leisure 1 *Dark Peak*.
Facilities	Pubs and cafés in Whaley Bridge. Café on the Sett Valley Trail (mentioned in text). Bike shop in Whaley Bridge.
Rail Access	Whaley Bridge Station.

Summary

A very good ride over varied and interesting terrain. It crosses high moorland with long climbs and descents, and can be quite arduous in poor conditions or windy weather. In low cloud the section approaching Mount Famine could give navigational problems. A good introduction to the joys of riding in the higher parts of the Peak.

The Route

Start in the carpark at the southern end of the Goyt Way in the centre of **Whaley Bridge**, OS grid ref. 012815. Leave the carpark and ride back out to the main A5004. Turn left, south, and ride for a few metres to take the first road right, west, just past the station. Pass under a railway bridge and immediately turn right again into Whaley Lane. Whaley Lane turns left and then climbs steadily.

After 1 km, turn right into Meadow Field (a road) and then immediately left into a narrower tarmac road. Do not go down the hill into the new estate. Follow the small road round and into a gravel lane. Traverse a short, muddy section and emerge on an open sloping hillside. Contour round the hill on a grassy terrace. The return route can be seen descending the hillside on the far side of the valley. Follow the bridleway as it curves leftwards round the hill. Ignore the track on the right that drops down to Hockley. Pass through a wooden gate to join a narrower track and follow this straight on. This enjoyable track ends at **Yeardsley Hall**. Go right and down past the Hall to reach the A6.

Cross straight over the A6 into Station Road. Ride down over a level crossing and the **River Goyt**. Just after the river the road makes a sharp left turn. 20 metres after the turn, take the steep, stone-stepped bridleway on the right. This soon becomes concrete surfaced and then meets a road. Turn right. Follow the road round to the left to pass under a double railway bridge. Ascend to the sharp right-hand bend. Leave the road by a gravel track on the left. After 50 metres follow the signposted bridleway to the left. Follow the track and a narrower, walled continuation past **Howcroft Farm**.

The track, a long steady climb, eventually joins a farm access track. Turn right and ride a few metres to a minor road near **Brownhill Farm**. Turn left, ride down the steep hill and round the left-hand bend. Where the road straightens and becomes less steep, go through a white metal gate on the right with a wooden stile next to it. Follow the grassy track straight up the field keeping the wall to your left. Carry straight on up beside a steep-sided gully to a gate. Go through the gate into the tarmac farmyard of **Hollinhurst Farm**. Follow the tarmac left to a T-junction.

Turn left and ride down the tarmac track past the quarry. One hundred metres past the quarry entrance, 7.8 km from the start of the ride, turn left into a gravel track, signposted *Cold Harbour Farm*. The surface becomes tarmac after a few metres and then the track forks. Take the right fork, over the cattle grid, and follow the tarmac down to **Over Lee Farm**. The bridleway continues to the left of the cottage and appears at first as if you are entering a private garden. Pass through the double wooden gates to the left of a small wooden gate with a name plate *Over Lee Cottage*. The lady in the cottage is very helpful but her dog is less so. Go straight on down a walled, grass track and continue beside the stream. This interesting descent is probably never dry, except perhaps – as on the original ride – when the ruts are frozen solid. A snorkel may by useful in really wet conditions. The track ends all to soon at a farm. Go straight on, ignoring the track to the right. Pass through a gate by a cottage and ride down to the A6015 on the outskirts of **New Mills**.

Turn left and ride for 100 metres before taking a bridleway on the right that drops into a field. This is marked by a tall wooden post. In the far corner of the field, meet tarmac and ride out to a minor road. Turn right. After 150 metres, and just before the sign for the village of Thornsett, pass through a gate on the right to join the **Sett Valley Trail**. Ride along the trail.

At a fork, 10.9 km from the start of the ride, a smaller path rises up to the right giving a choice of routes.

If you go down to the left you reach the road and a café. If you go up to the right you will cross straight over the road and continue on the trail. If you do choose the café you can rejoin the trail by crossing over the road, riding up right for a few metres and then passing through a gate on the left to take the track that climbs beside the road.

Whichever route you choose, they will meet at a gate on the far side of the road. Continue along the trail for approximately 300 metres. After 300 metres, about 11.3 km from the start, turn right and climb a short, steep path to the A6015 on the outskirts of **Hayfield**. Go straight across into **Morland Road**.

It is a long pull up this broken tarmac track. Rest assured that in retrospect you will really enjoy having overcome this challenging ascent! At the left-hand bend go straight on and leave the track by a gate. Follow the bridleway, signposted on a weather-beaten fingerpost *Chinley via Chinley Church*, as it climbs the moor next to a wall. Where the wall turns to the left, marked by a bridleway signpost, turn left and follow the wall downhill. Ignore two vague bridleways that branch off to the right, but follow the broken path down to a bridlegate. After the gate a narrow path descends through silver birch woodland. This enjoyable descent ends at a gate above and behind a barn at **Phoside Farm**. Turn left and then right through a wooden gate with an old barrel beside it, to emerge in front of the barn. Descend the gravel track to the **A624**.

Go straight across into a tarmac bridleway. Ride up the bridleway for a short distance to a minor road. Turn left to ride down the hill. Ignore the first tempting looking track on the right – which is, unfortunately, a footpath. Ride down Highgate Road to take, about 14.5 km from the start, the first minor road on the right; Valley Road. Follow Valley Road as it curves left to pass in front of a long terrace of gritstone houses. Stay on Valley Road as it parallels the river, ignoring various roads to the right.

Soon the road gives way to a gravel track. Follow this track beside the river to a fork by two large, square stone-capped pillars, where a footpath leaves the track. Take the bridleway right, signposted *Kinderlow and Edale*. Follow this track up past **Stones House**.

For a short section the surface deteriorates to rubble, making riding very tricky. Continue skirting the edge of the wood, climbing to a bridlegate where another bridleway joins from the right. Go through the gate and follow the path diagonally down across the field to a tarmac track. Turn right and, after 150 metres, leave the track for the obvious track on the right that climbs steadily across the open fields towards Mount Famine. The track forks; take the right fork up the track that soon fades into the open hillside. Continue upwards heading for the obvious nick in the skyline between Mount Famine on the left and a small rocky hill on the right.

At the nick, pass through the gate and carry straight on over and down the rough fields, keeping close to the wall on the right. Enter a fenced section of bridleway and follow it down, across a track and into a wider, walled bridleway. This leads down to the **A624** road.

Turn left. After 100 metres turn right towards **Peep-O-Day**. Ride up the tarmac drive and then straight on through the gate to a bridleway junction. Go straight on, signposted *Birch Vale via Grouse Inn*. Follow the track straight on over another track that crosses your path.

At a fork in the path, go left and ride down to join a cinder track which then climbs steeply to **Higher Hills Cottage**. Pass to the left of the cottage and then follow the narrower path as it curves to the right, behind the cottage. Climb up to the moor, pass through a gate,

Cobbled bridleway near Hollinhurst Farm.

and carry straight on, riding between broken dry-stone walls. Follow this track over rough moorland to a bridleway junction. Take the track left that continues between the walls.

Meander across the moor on this interesting rocky track. Carry straight on where a footpath and bridleway cross your route, then begin the long descent into Whaley Bridge. The bridleway eventually becomes a rutted farm track which eventually meets a tarmac road.

Turn right then take the first minor road left. Turn left again at a T-junction and ride down to another T-junction with the **B6062** at **Brierley Green**. Turn right.

Follow the **B6062** down for 2 km to a sharp left-hand bend and then after another 200 metres to a junction with the **A6**. Turn left and ride to a roundabout. Turn right, signposted (*B5470*) *Macclesfield & Whaley Bridge*, and ride for 600 metres back to the carpark where the ride started.

INFORMATION

The Off-road Code

Only ride where you have the legal right to do so.

Always yield to horses and pedestrians.

Avoid animals and crops. In some circumstances this may not be possible, at which times contact should be kept to a minimum.

Take all litter with you.

Leave all gates as found.

Keep noise down.

Don't get annoyed with anyone, it never solves any problems.

Always try to be self sufficient, for you and your bike.

Never create a fire hazard.

The Country Code

Enjoy the countryside and respect its life and work.

Guard against all fire risks.

Fasten all gates.

Keep your dogs under close control.

Keep to public paths across farmland.

Use gates and stiles to cross fences, hedges and walls.

Leave livestock, crops and machinery alone.

Take your litter home.

Help keep water clean.

Protect wildlife, plants and trees.

Take special care on country roads.

Make no unnecessary noise.

Use your common sense where these codes seem to contradict each other.